HOW TO FILE YOUR OWN BANKRUPTCY

(or How to Avoid It)

with forms

Edward A. Haman
Attorney at Law

Sphinx Publishing
A Division of Sourcebooks, Inc.
Naperville, IL • Clearwater, FL

Fourth edition, 1998

Published by: **Sourcebooks, Inc.**

Naperville Office
P.O. Box 372
Naperville, Illinois 60566
(630) 961-3900
FAX: 630-961-2168

Clearwater Office
P.O. Box 25
Clearwater, Florida 33757
(813) 587-0999
FAX: 813-586-5088

Cover Design: Andrew Sardina/Dominique Raccah, Sourcebooks, Inc.
Interior Design and Production: Andrew Sardina, Sourcebooks, Inc.

This publication is designed to provide accurate and authoritative information in regard to the subject matter covered. It is sold with the understanding that the publisher is not engaged in rendering legal, accounting, or other professional service. If legal advice or other expert assistance is required, the services of a competent professional person should be sought.

From a Declaration of Principles Jointly Adopted by a Committee of the
American Bar Association and a Committee of Publishers and Associations

Library of Congress Cataloging-in-Publication Data
Haman, Edward A.
    How to file your own bankruptcy (or how to avoid it) : with forms / Edward A. Haman.—4th ed.
      p. cm.
    Includes index.
      ISBN 1-57071-223-9 (pbk.)
      1. Bankruptcy—United States—Popular works.   2. Bankruptcy—United States—Forms. I. Title.
    KF 1524.6.H36   1997
    346.7307'8—dc21   97-18428
                                                                                          CIP

Printed and bound in the United States of America.

Paperback — 10 9 8 7 6 5 4 3 2

CONTENTS

USING SELF-HELP LAW BOOKS 1

INTRODUCTION 3

SECTION 1: BANKRUPTCY AND THE LEGAL SYSTEM 5
    What is Bankruptcy?
    The Legal System
    Bankruptcy Law and Procedure

SECTION 2: LAWYERS 17
    Do You Want a Lawyer?
    Selecting a Lawyer
    Working with a Lawyer

SECTION 3: CAN YOU AVOID BANKRUPTCY? 25
    The Effects of Bankruptcy
    Income and Expense Worksheet (Form 1)
    Property Worksheet (Form 2)
    Debt Worksheet (Form 3)
    General Guidelines
    Alternatives to Bankruptcy

SECTION 4: ARRANGING YOUR FINANCES 45
    Incurring New Debts
    Sell Non-Exempt Property and Buy Exempt Property
    Sell Non-Exempt Property and Pay Certain Debts
    Defrauding Creditors (*Don't!*)

SECTION 5: GATHERING INFORMATION 49
    Income
    Expenses
    Property
    Debts
    Legal Research

SECTION 6: COURT FORMS 55
    Understanding Legal Forms
    Voluntary Petition (Form 4)
    Application to Pay Filing Fee in Installments (Form 5)
    Schedule A—Real Property (Form 7)
    Schedule B—Personal Property (Form 8)
    Schedule C—Property Claimed as Exempt (Form 9)
    Schedule D—Creditors Holding Secured Claims (Form 10)
    Schedule E—Creditors Holding Unsecured Priority Claims (Form 11)
    Schedule F—Creditors Holding Unsecured Nonpriority Claims (Form 12)
    Schedule G—Executory Contracts and Unexpired Leases (Form 13)
    Schedule H—Codebtors (Form 14)
    Schedule I—Current Income of Individual Debtor(s) (Form 15)
    Schedule J—Current Expenditures of Individual Debtor(s) (Form 16)
    Summary of Schedules (Form 6)
    Declaration Concerning Debtor's Schedules (Form 17)
    Statement of Financial Affairs (Form 18)
    Chapter 7 Individual Debtor's Statement of Intention (Form 19)
    Chapter 13 Plan (Form 20)
    Mailing Matrix (Form 21)

SECTION 7: COURT PROCEDURES 77
    Filing with the Court Clerk, Etc.
    Creditors' Meeting
    Court Hearing and Discharge

SECTION 8: SPECIAL CIRCUMSTANCES 85
    Amending Your Paperwork
    Changing from Chapter 13 to Chapter 7
    Lien Avoidance
    Redemption
    Reaffirming a Debt
    Lawsuits
    Pensions and Retirement Plans

SECTION 9: AFTER YOUR DISCHARGE 91
    Handling Your Finances
    Obtaining Credit (If You Dare!)

APPENDIX A: EXEMPTIONS (FEDERAL AND STATE-BY-STATE) 95

APPENDIX B: FORMS 151

INDEX 197

Using Self-Help Law Books

Whenever you shop for a product or service, you are faced with various levels of quality and price. In deciding what product or service to buy, you make a cost/value analysis on the basis of your willingness to pay and the quality you desire.

When buying a car, you decide whether you want transportation, comfort, status, or sex appeal. Accordingly, you decide among such choices as a Neon, a Lincoln, a Rolls Royce, or a Porsche. Before making a decision, you usually weigh the merits of each option against the cost.

When you get a headache, you can take a pain reliever (such as aspirin) or go visit a medical specialist for a neurological examination. Given this choice, most people, of course, take a pain reliever, since it costs only pennies, whereas a medical examination costs hundreds of dollars and takes a lot of time. This is usually a logical choice because rarely is anything more than a pain reliever needed for a headache. But in some cases, a headache may indicate a brain tumor, and failing to see a specialist right away can result in complications. Should everyone with a headache go to a specialist? Of course not, but people treating their own illnesses must realize that they are betting on the basis of their cost/value analysis of the situation, they are taking the most logical option.

The same cost/value analysis must be made in deciding to do one's own legal work. Many legal situations are very straight forward, requiring a simple form and no complicated analysis. Anyone with a little intelligence and a book of instructions can handle the matter without outside help.

But there is always the chance that complications are involved that only an attorney would notice. To simplify the law into a book like this, several legal cases often must be condensed into a single sentence or paragraph. Otherwise, the book would be several hundred pages long and too complicated for most people. However, this simplification necessarily leaves out many details and nuances that would apply to special or unusual situations. Also, there are many ways to interpret most legal questions. Your case may come before a judge who disagrees with the analysis of our authors.

Therefore, in deciding to use a self-help law book and to do your own legal work, you must realize that you are making a cost/value analysis and deciding that the chance your case will not turn out to your satisfaction is outweighed by the money you will save in doing it yourself. Most people handling their own simple legal matters never have a problem, but occasionally people find that it ended up costing them more to have an attorney straighten out the situation than it would have if they had hired an attorney in the beginning. Keep this in mind while handling your case, and be sure to consult an attorney if you feel you might need further guidance.

INTRODUCTION

Is this book for you? You are probably feeling burdened by your financial situation, or else you wouldn't be reading this. If you are like most Americans, you are probably struggling to make payments on a mortgage, car loan, medical bills, various credit cards, and possibly a student loan, home improvement loan, or other consumer debts. This book is designed specifically for you. It will help you analyze your situation, decide whether you should file for bankruptcy, and guide you through the steps to either avoid bankruptcy or get through the bankruptcy procedure. This is not a law school course, but a practical guide to get you through "the system" as easily as possible.

This book presents fairly simplified procedures for use by non-attorneys. It does not contain all the possible loopholes or tricks of the trade that an experienced bankruptcy lawyer might use to gain a little extra advantage. On the other hand, for many people, these legal details either don't apply, or their advantage will be offset by not having to pay the fee of an experienced bankruptcy attorney.

If you are at a high income level, or have extensive and complicated investments and debts, you will need a lawyer. However, this book will still help you to understand the system and work with your lawyer more effectively.

This book is not designed for corporate, partnership, or business-related bankruptcies.

Bankruptcy law is covered in various chapters of the federal Bankruptcy Code. This book covers bankruptcy under Chapter 7 and Chapter 13 of the Bankruptcy Code. In order to avoid confusion between chapters of the Bankruptcy Code and what would normally be called chapters of this book, the word section will be used instead of the word chapter when referring to this book. The word chapter will only be used when referring to the Bankruptcy Code.

Sections 1 through 5 of this book will explain the legal system, help you decide if bankruptcy is for you, and help you prepare for filing for bankruptcy. Section 6 will explain what forms you need and how to prepare them. Section 7 explains the bankruptcy court procedures. Section 8 deals with special circumstances that may arise, and section 9 gives you some advice for the future once you have completed your bankruptcy case in court. Appendix A contains the federal and state lists of property that you may keep even if you file for bankruptcy, and appendix B contains the forms you will need.

Be sure to read this entire book, especially section 6 on "Understanding Legal Forms," before you begin preparing any of the forms in this book. You may want to make several copies of the forms in this book, and save the originals in order to make more copies if you need them.

BANKRUPTCY AND THE LEGAL SYSTEM 1

WHAT IS BANKRUPTCY?

Simply stated, bankruptcy is a legal procedure that allows you to get out of oppressive debt, and get a fresh start financially. The concept of bankruptcy goes back at least to the time of the Old Testament, where it states: "At the end of every seven years you shall grant a release and this is the manner of the release: every creditor shall release what he has lent to his neighbor…" (Deuteronomy 15:1-2).

In the United States, the importance of bankruptcy was recognized at the time of our nation's birth, and was made a part of the U.S. Constitution. Article I, Section 8 of the U.S. Constitution gives Congress the power to establish "uniform laws on the subject of bankruptcies throughout the United States." In 1800, Congress enacted the first bankruptcy laws.

Today, there exists a comprehensive set of federal laws that govern bankruptcy. There are so many bankruptcies filed each year that there is a special division of the federal court system devoted exclusively to bankruptcy. In recent years, bankruptcy filings have reached over one-million annually. So if you need to file for bankruptcy, you can be sure you will not be alone! The bankruptcy procedure serves two purposes.

First, it allows you to change your financial situation. Second, it gets your creditors off your back while you make this change.

You also have a choice about changing your situation. You can choose either of two procedures. The first is traditional bankruptcy, where your debts are forgiven altogether. The other procedure is referred to as a *re-organization, wage-earner plan,* or *payment plan.* In this procedure, you arrange to pay off some or all of your debts according to a payment plan that you can handle on your income. Although this is technically not bankruptcy, it is a part of the bankruptcy law and will be referred to in this book as a bankruptcy.

Traditional bankruptcy is covered in Chapter 7 of the federal Bankruptcy Code, and is often referred to as a *Chapter 7.* The payment plan procedure is covered in Chapter 13 of the Bankruptcy Code, and is referred to as a *Chapter 13.* These procedures will be discussed in greater detail in later sections of this book. (When referring to parts of this book, the word *section* will be used instead of the word *chapter,* to help avoid confusion with chapters of the Bankruptcy Code.)

There are other chapters to the Bankruptcy Code. *Chapter 12* is specially designed for farmers, so if you are a farmer you should consult a bankruptcy lawyer. *Chapter 11* is generally designed for corporations and partnerships. Chapter 11 is also available to individuals, although it is not used unless the person has secured debts in excess of $350,000, unsecured debts in excess of $100,000, and sufficient income to pay off a portion of these debts over several years. If you are in this situation you should consult a lawyer, or a book that covers Chapter 11 bankruptcies.

THE LEGAL SYSTEM

This section will give you a general introduction to the legal system of the bankruptcy court. Most people have an idea of the way the legal system *should* be, which usually does not match the realities of the system.

If you don't learn to accept the realities, you will experience much stress and frustration. Although bankruptcy can get as complicated as any other area of law, for most cases it is a bit more cut and dried and predictable than many other areas.

RULES
Our legal system is a system of rules. There are basically three types of rules:

1. Rules of Law: These provide the basic substance of the law, such as defining a debt and describing what property can be kept after bankruptcy.

2. Rules of Procedure: These outline how matters are to be handled in the courts, such as requiring court papers to be in a certain form, or filed within a certain time.

3. Rules of Evidence: These set forth the manner in which facts are to be proven.

In bankruptcy it is not usually necessary to be concerned with rules of evidence, which automatically makes this an easier area of the law. In addition, the rules of law and procedure are so well defined that, in most cases, they are not nearly as complicated and subject to interpretation as in many other areas. For most middle-class Americans, bankruptcy is mostly filling out certain forms, filing them with the court, and attending a couple of meetings. As long as you provide the court with accurate and complete information about your finances, you shouldn't have any difficulties.

A basic rule of this book is *don't panic!* If, as you read, you find yourself thinking "I'll never be able to do this myself," *keep reading*. By the end of the book you'll see that it is really a fairly simple matter.

The advice "don't panic" also applies to dealing with the court. The United States is divided into numerous districts, and each district has its own bankruptcy court. Each court has a court clerk, and may have some local rules. It is possible that the clerk in your district will tell you that one of your papers is not exactly correct in its form or content. This happens to lawyers with many years of experience, so there is no need to feel bad if it happens to you. If this happens to you, all you can do is relax, find out exactly what the clerk wants, and do it the clerk's way. Similar to the old saying about the Army, there is the right way, the wrong way, and the clerk's way. Only the clerk's way will get you what you want. Fortunately, the forms are standardized all over the country, so this should not be a problem.

THE SYSTEM

Although bankruptcy is relatively simple and straight-forward, there are a few realities of our nation's legal system that can apply to all areas of the law to some degree. A brief mention of these realities may prepare you in the event you come across any of them.

The system is not perfect. The rules are designed to apply to all persons in all situations. This can sometimes lead to an unfair result. An example relates to the federal Employee Retirement Income Security Act (*ERISA*), which was designed to assure that certain retirement benefits are preserved. In applying a general legal principal, that the existence of complete federal laws prohibit states from making laws on the same subject, the U.S. Supreme Court ruled that states can't make laws that give even more protection to these ERISA benefits. This ridiculous ruling was later reversed, but only after causing problems for numerous people. It is also possible for a judge to make a bad call, or for someone to cheat and not get caught (such as by not telling the truth even under oath). As a well-known and respected judge once said to the young attorney: "This is a court of law, young man, not a court of justice!"

Judges don't always follow the rules. This is a shocking discovery for many young lawyers. After spending three years in law school learning legal theory, and after spending countless hours preparing for a hearing in which all of the law is on your side, you find that the judge isn't going to pay any attention to legal theories and the law. As one judge is known to have put it: "In my courtroom, the law is what I say it is." Many decisions are made simply on the judge's personal view of what seems fair under the circumstances (even if the judge doesn't take the time to fully understand the circumstances, and even if he or she has a strange idea of fairness). The judge will then find some way to try to justify his or her decision, even if it means distorting or ignoring the existing law.

The system is slow. Even lawyers get frustrated at how long it can take to get a case completed (especially if they don't get paid until it is finished). Things generally take longer than you would expect. Patience is required to get through the system with a minimum of stress. Don't get angry and let your frustration show.

No two cases are alike. If your friends or co-workers learn that you've filed for bankruptcy, you can be sure you will be getting much "legal" advice from them. *Don't listen to them!* Everyone has their own experience to relate, or a story to tell about a friend or relative who has gone through bankruptcy. *Don't listen to them!* They probably used an attorney, and attorneys are not always good about explaining the law and procedure to their clients. The attitude of many attorneys is: "I know what I'm doing, trust me, you don't need to know all of the legal details." After reading this book, you will know more about bankruptcy than any of your friends. You will also know more than some attorneys! Also, your case is not exactly the same as the one they will want to tell you about, so you can't expect your experience will be the same.

THE PLAYERS   Law and the legal system are often compared to games, and just like games, it is important to understand who the players are.

The judge. The judge has the power to determine whether your debts can be discharged (or whether your payment plan is accepted). In bankruptcy court, the judge is a U.S. District Court Judge, who is appointed to his position for life by the President. Bankruptcy judges have large caseloads, and like it best when your case can be conducted quickly and without hassles. This means that you want to be sure that your papers are completed correctly, with complete and accurate information. Most likely, you will only see the judge at your final hearing, which will only take a few minutes. The most important thing is to show respect for the judge. This means that you will answer the judge's questions as simply and to the point as possible. Under no circumstances will you get into an argument with the judge, or with a creditor while you are before the judge. You will always follow the judge's instructions without argument or complaint.

The court clerk. The job of the clerk is to handle the filing of papers, the scheduling of hearings, and the maintaining of the court's files. Be sure you are friendly and cooperative toward the people in the clerk's office. If you make a clerk your enemy there is no end to the trouble he or she can cause you. Generally, the clerk has no interest in the outcome of your case, but is only interested that all of the paperwork is in order. The clerk has the power to accept or reject your papers. If the clerk wants something changed in your papers, just find out what he or she wants, and do it. If you happen to come across a particularly unfriendly clerk— try to understand that clerks frequently deal with frustrated, angry and rude people. You'll get much better treatment by showing the clerk that you are happy to cooperate and are patient with the slowness of the system, rather than being just another rude person causing him or her stress.

The trustee. After you file your first papers, your case will be assigned to a trustee. The trustee's job is to make sure that your papers are complete and accurate, assure that all of your creditors are notified about your bankruptcy, handle the disposition of your assets, and generally assure that your case continues properly and is ready for final hearing with the judge. The trustee works for the court, and is a middle-man between you, your creditors, and the court.

The creditors. These are the people and companies that you owe money. These people will not be happy about your bankruptcy, because it means they will probably not get paid. Some of them may get to take back the property they sold you, and some of them will get nothing. Some of them may be very hostile, and some of them will just accept your bankruptcy as part of the risk of doing business (after all, they encouraged you to buy on credit). Once you file for bankruptcy your creditors can no longer bother you for payment. You may stop making payments once you file, except on items you don't want to lose (such as your home and car). All your creditor can do is either object to the court that you don't qualify for bankruptcy, or object to your plan for how their debt is to be handled. In most cases, neither objection meets with much success.

Lawyers. This either refers to your lawyer (which will be discussed more in section 4 of this book), or to your creditor's lawyer. Generally, in bankruptcy proceedings there will be little difference between dealing with your creditor or his attorney. Many lawyers are dignified and polite in their dealings with the other side in a case. These lawyers will try to get the best deal for their client, and will do it in a polite and honest, but firm and business-like, manner. Other lawyers are truly nasty people, who are impolite and can't deal with their opponent in a civilized manner. They will not hesitate to make threats and lie about the law in an attempt to intimidate you. These lawyers simply can't be reasoned with, and you shouldn't try. If you encounter one of these lawyers, simply don't speak to him or her. Just address all of your statements to the trustee or the judge instead (very respectfully and politely of course). If you are uncertain of the law as stated by such an attorney, you may wish to consult an attorney yourself.

BANKRUPTCY LAW AND PROCEDURE

IN GENERAL

This section will give you a summary of the law and the procedure of bankruptcy. We will get into the details and the "how to" later, but first it is important to get a more general and overall view of the process.

The idea of the bankruptcy law is to give you a fresh start, free from your previous debts, with enough assets to live on and get you started again. The law sets up different classes of debts and property, which determine what property you can keep, what property you can't keep, and whether and how much your creditors get paid.

SIX-YEAR
LIMITATION

There are some limits as to how often you can use bankruptcy. You may not file under Chapter 7 if (1) you obtained a discharge under a

Chapter 7, 11, 12 or 13 petition filed within the past six years, (2) you had a Chapter 7 case dismissed within the past 180 days because you violated a court order, or (3) you had a Chapter 7 case dismissed within the past 180 days because you asked for dismissal after a creditor asked for the automatic stay to be lifted. However, these limits do not apply to Chapter 13 cases, which may be filed at any time. If your secured debts exceed $350,000, or your unsecured debts exceed $100,000, you may not use Chapter 13. If you are in this situation, you should consult a lawyer, or a book that covers filing under Chapter 11 of the Bankruptcy Code.

EXEMPT AND NON-EXEMPT PROPERTY

Each piece of property you own will be classified as either *exempt* (which means you may be able to keep it), or as *non-exempt* (which means you will have to turn it over to the trustee). Although the Bankruptcy Code is a federal law, the available exemptions are different in each state. Appendix A of this book will tell you how to determine the property that is exempt in your state, and this will be discussed in more detail later. Most states will allow you to keep a certain dollar value of real estate, a car, tools used in your profession, insurance policies, clothing, household furnishings, retirement benefits, public benefits (such as workers' compensation and unemployment), and other personal items. These are exempt property. However, exempt property may still be lost if you borrowed money to buy it and don't keep up your payments.

SECURED AND UNSECURED DEBTS

This brings us to the classification of debts as either *secured* or *unsecured*. A secured debt is one that is covered by a certain piece of property. The most common examples are home mortgages and car loans. The papers you signed when you borrowed the money specifically state that if you don't pay, the lender may take the property. You may not keep such property unless you pay for it, even if it would otherwise be exempt property in your state. So, if you don't want to lose your home or car, you will have to arrange a payment plan acceptable to your lender, or just keep your payments current.

An unsecured debt is not covered by any property. Examples of unsecured debts are a department store credit card, a VISA card, and medical bills. In these cases, the lender does not get paid and does not get any property either. Even if you bought your dining room furniture with your credit card, it is still an unsecured debt (unless you also signed some additional paper that states that the property secured the loan).

NON-
DISCHARGEABLE
DEBTS

One other significant part of the law is that there are a few types of debts that cannot be discharged in bankruptcy. The four most common types of non-dischargeable debts are—taxes (with certain exceptions), government guaranteed student loans, child support, and alimony. So even if you go through a bankruptcy, you will still have to pay these debts.

BANKRUPTCY
PROCEDURE

The bankruptcy procedure can be viewed as a simple four-step process:

1. You prepare and file your VOLUNTARY PETITION (Form 4) and various supporting documents. This is simply a request for the court to discharge your debts (or approve your payment plan) according to the law, and information about your income, expenses, property and debts.

2. The trustee sends notices to all of your creditors to advise them that you have filed for bankruptcy. This gives them an opportunity to be sure you have given correct information in your VOLUNTARY PETITION, and to raise any questions or objections.

3. You have a meeting with the trustee and your creditors (if they show up). This is when any questions or objections are discussed and settled.

4. You attend a hearing, at which time the judge will discharge your debts (or approve your payment plan). This may even be a mass-discharge of many cases at one time, in which you and many others obtain a discharge at the same time.

OTHER
CONSIDERATIONS

You should also consider the following things before you decide to file for bankruptcy:

☞ If a friend or relative co-signed a loan for you, that friend or relative will still be liable for the debt.

☞ You may have your case dismissed if the judge determines that you have enough income to pay your debts, if you defrauded your creditors, or if you charged a lot for entertainment, vacations, or luxury items just before filing.

☞ You may not need to file for bankruptcy if your only goal is to get bill collectors off your back, or to avoid having your property or wages attached. Other state and federal laws may be able to accomplish these goals without filing for bankruptcy.

CHAPTER 7
BANKRUPTCY
(DISCHARGE OF
DEBTS)

As mentioned earlier, there are two types of bankruptcy for individuals: the discharge of debts, and the payment plan. Chapter 7 of the Bankruptcy Code is for the discharge of debts, which is the traditional bankruptcy. This is where you either pay for, or give up, your property for secured debts. You will surrender any non-exempt property in order to pay off as much of your other debt as possible. You will keep all of your other exempt property, and will be forever released from any obligation to repay the remaining debt.

One important requirement for a Chapter 7 bankruptcy is that you don't have enough income to allow you to pay your debts. If the judge finds that you have enough income, he will dismiss your case. This will be discussed in more detail in a later section of this book.

CHAPTER 13
BANKRUPTCY
(PAYMENT PLAN)

In a Chapter 13 bankruptcy you are not seeking to get rid of all of your debt entirely, but only to do one or a combination of the following:

1. Restructure your payments so that they are more manageable considering your income.

2. Get rid of part of your debt so that you can manage payments again.

This can be done by spreading your payments over a longer period of time, or by paying only a part of the loan. Either way your monthly or weekly payment will be reduced. This type of payment plan can last up to three years, which means your finances will be under the watchful eye of the trustee during this time.

The two main things the trustee and the judge will consider in deciding whether to accept your plan are whether the creditors are being treated fairly, and whether each creditor will receive at least as much as if you had gone with the traditional Chapter 7 bankruptcy.

For a Chapter 13 bankruptcy you will fill out some different forms than for a Chapter 7. The main difference is that you will need to fill out a form in which you offer a payment plan that you create. In a Chapter 13 case the creditors' meeting is usually concerned with trying to reach a plan that will be acceptable to the creditors. So you may spend some time negotiating with the creditors as they try to get you to change your plan so they get more money or get it faster. It is not necessary that the creditors agree with your plan, but if they do agree it will be easily accepted by the trustee and the judge. Even if the creditors object to your plan, it will still be approved as long as it is fair (in the judge's opinion of what is fair, which usually relates to all creditors of the same type being treated equally), and as long as each creditor gets at least as much as if you had filed under Chapter 7.

CONVERTING TO ANOTHER CHAPTER

It is also possible for you to convert to a Chapter 7 bankruptcy, if you later determine this is a better solution to your debt problems. It is also possible to convert a Chapter 7 to a Chapter 13 case, although this is not usually done unless the judge determines that you have enough income to pay off your debts over a few years and is about to dismiss your case. Most people will find that they have less income to go around, therefore requiring a Chapter 7. Only if you find that your income is sufficient to enable you to pay off most of your debts within three years would you consider changing to a Chapter 13.

LAWYERS 2

You are not required to have a lawyer in order to file for bankruptcy. Most people should be able to handle their own bankruptcy. You will probably need an attorney if:

- ☛ You are involved in a business, either alone or in a partnership.

- ☛ You own stock in a privately held corporation.

- ☛ You are married and your spouse is not filing for bankruptcy with you.

- ☛ You are a farmer. (There are special bankruptcy laws covering farm bankruptcy.)

- ☛ You encounter a creditor, trustee, or judge who is particularly difficult.

DO YOU WANT A LAWYER?

No doubt, one of your first questions about bankruptcy is: How much will an attorney cost? Attorneys come in all price ranges. Most attorneys will charge between $750 and $1,500, depending upon where you live and the complexity of your case. Ads for $150 to $200 bankruptcies are usually only available in very simple cases, and are "no frills" services. If you use one of these lawyers, just be sure you know exactly what will be provided for the fee. The lawyer will usually want to be paid in advance. Most new (and therefore less expensive) attorneys would be quite capable of handling a simple bankruptcy, but, by the time you've read this book, you will probably know as much about bankruptcy as most of these new attorneys.

ADVANTAGES TO HAVING A LAWYER

The following are some reasons why you may want to consider hiring a lawyer:

☛ You may be able to save more of your property. A lawyer may be able to find more loopholes in the bankruptcy law, or give you other suggestions, which will preserve more assets or discharge more debt. However, these savings may be offset by the attorney's fee you will need to pay. Generally, the more loopholes you want, the more experienced (and expensive) of an attorney you will need.

☛ Judges and other attorneys may take you more seriously. People who represent themselves often waste time by being unfamiliar with the procedures. However, this should not be a problem with anyone who has read this book.

☛ A lawyer can serve as a buffer between you and your creditors.

☛ In the event your case becomes complicated, it is an advantage to have an attorney who is familiar with your case. It can be comforting to have a lawyer for advice and reassurance. Again, the more advice and reassurance, the higher the attorney's fee will rise.

ADVANTAGES TO REPRESENTING YOURSELF

Here are some reasons why you may want to do the work yourself:

☛ You save the cost of a lawyer.

☛ Sometimes judges and trustees feel more sympathetic toward a person who is not represented by a lawyer. Often they will actually help you.

☞ The procedure may be faster. One of the most frequent complaints about lawyers involves delay in completing the case, usually due to heavy caseloads. If you are handling your own case, you will be able to keep it moving through the system.

☞ Selecting a good attorney is not easy.

MIDDLE
GROUND

You may want to look for an attorney who will be willing to accept an hourly fee to answer your questions and give you help on an as needed basis. Expect to pay at least $75 per hour for such consultation. Attorneys offering "free initial consultation," or a consultation "for just $20," will often not provide you with any usable advice, or explain how you should do something.

SELECTING A LAWYER

FINDING
LAWYERS

Finding a lawyer is a two-step process. First, you need to decide which attorney (or attorneys) to make an appointment with, then you need to decide if you want to hire that attorney.

☞ *Ask a friend.* A common, and frequently the best, way to find a lawyer is to ask someone you know to recommend one.

☞ *Lawyer Referral Service.* You can find a referral service by looking in the Yellow Pages of your phone directory under the heading "Attorney Referral Services" or "Attorneys." The referral service is free, but it does not guarantee the quality of the attorney's work, nor the level of experience or ability.

☞ *Yellow Pages.* Check under the heading for "Attorneys." Look for ads for firms or lawyers that indicate they handle bankruptcy or credit matters.

☞ *Newspaper.* In the classified ads you should find a section for "Legal Services," that often includes the least expensive attorneys. But expect minimal services. You may even be given a set of forms to complete yourself!

☛ Ask another lawyer. If you have used an attorney in the past (such as for a will, real estate closing or traffic ticket), call him or her and ask for a referral to a bankruptcy attorney.

EVALUATING A LAWYER

You should select three to five lawyers worthy of further consideration. Call each attorney's office and ask the following questions:

☛ Does the attorney (or firm) handle bankruptcies?

☛ How much can you expect it to cost?

☛ How soon can you get an appointment?

☛ What is the cost for an initial consultation?

If you like the answers you get, ask if you can speak to the attorney. Once you get in contact with the attorney (either by phone or at an appointment), ask the following questions:

☛ How much will it cost?

☛ How will the fee be paid? (Usually it is paid in advance, in full.)

☛ What percentage of the attorney's cases involve bankruptcies? (Don't expect an exact answer, but you should get a rough estimate of at least 10%).

☛ How long will it take? (Don't expect an exact answer, but the attorney should be able to give you an average range and discuss the variables.)

If you get acceptable answers to these questions, it's time to ask yourself these questions:

☛ Do I feel comfortable talking to this lawyer?

☛ Does this lawyer seem confident?

☛ Is this lawyer willing and able to explain things so I can understand?

If you get satisfactory answers to all of these questions, you probably have a lawyer you'll be able to work with. Remember, you are interviewing the lawyer to see if you want to hire him.

WORKING WITH A LAWYER

You will most likely work best with your attorney if you keep an open, honest and friendly attitude. You should also consider the following suggestions:

Ask questions. If you want to know something, or if you don't understand something, ask your attorney. If you don't understand the answer, ask him or her to explain it again. There are many points of law that even lawyers don't fully understand, so you shouldn't be embarrassed to ask questions. If your lawyer won't take the time to explain what he or she is doing, it may be time to look for a new lawyer.

Give your lawyer complete information. Anything you tell your lawyer is confidential, and your lawyer can't help you if he or she doesn't have all of the information.

Accept reality. Accept what your lawyer tells you about the law and the system. It is pointless to argue because the law or the system doesn't work the way you think it should. Remember, it's not your lawyer's fault that the system isn't perfect, or that the law doesn't say what you'd like it to say.

Be patient. Be patient with the system, as well as with your attorney. Don't expect your attorney to return your phone call within an hour. Your attorney may not be able to return it the same day either. Most lawyers are very busy. It is rare that an attorney can maintain a full caseload and still make each client feel as if he is the only client.

Talk to the secretary. Your lawyer's secretary can be a valuable source of information. So be friendly and get to know him or her. Often the secretary will be able to answer your questions and you won't get a bill for the time you talk. Even if the secretary can't answer your question, he or she can probably get the answer from the attorney and call you back faster than if you insist on waiting to speak directly to the lawyer.

Be on time. This applies to appointments with your lawyer, and to court hearings.

Keep your case moving. Many lawyers operate on the old principal of the squeaking wheel gets the oil. Work on a case tends to get put off until a deadline is near, an emergency develops, or the client calls. There is a reason for this. Many lawyers take more cases than can be effectively handled in order to increase their income. Your task is to become a squeaking wheel, but one that doesn't squeak to the point of being aggravating to your lawyer and his or her office staff. Whenever you talk to your lawyer, ask him or her the following questions:

☛ What is the next step?

☛ When do you expect it to be done?

☛ When should I talk to you next?

If you don't hear from the lawyer when you expect, call him or her the following day. Don't remind your lawyer that you didn't receive a call; just ask how your case is going.

How to save money. Of course you don't want to spend unnecessary money for an attorney. Here are a few things you can do to avoid excess legal fees:

☛ Don't make unnecessary phone calls to your lawyer.

☛ Give information to the secretary whenever possible.

☛ Direct questions to the secretary first.

☞ Plan phone calls so you get to the point. Write down an outline if necessary.

☞ Do some of the legwork yourself—pick up and deliver papers, for example. Ask what you can do to assist your lawyer.

☞ Be prepared for appointments. Have all related papers with you, plan your visit to get to the point. Make an outline of what you want to discuss and ask.

Firing your lawyer. If you find that you can no longer work with your lawyer, or don't trust your lawyer, it is time to either go it alone or get a new attorney. You will need to send your lawyer a letter stating that you no longer desire his or her services and are discharging him or her from your case. Also state that you will be coming by his or her office the following day to pick up your file. The attorney does not have to give you his or her own notes or other work in progress, but your lawyer must give you the essential contents of your file (such as copies of papers already prepared and billed for, and any documents you provided). If your attorney refuses to give you your file for any reason, contact your state's bar association about filing a complaint or *grievance* against the lawyer. Of course, you will need to settle any remaining fees owed.

CAN YOU AVOID BANKRUPTCY? 3

THE EFFECTS OF BANKRUPTCY

Bankruptcy should be regarded as a last resort. Before you jump into a bankruptcy, it is a good idea to evaluate your financial situation, and consider the effects of a bankruptcy. Before you make a final decision, be sure to look at section 8 of this book to see if any of the special circumstances discussed there apply to you.

FINANCIAL EFFECTS

A bankruptcy is a mixed blessing. It will have both positive and negative financial effects. These can be divided into immediate and long-term effects.

Immediate effects. An immediate positive effect is that your creditors will get off your back. However, this may only last a short time for certain kinds of debts. Such things as utility cut-offs, mortgage foreclosures, or evictions, may only be delayed for a few days or weeks. Once you file for bankruptcy, your financial dealings come under the scrutiny of the bankruptcy trustee. You will need his permission to sell any assets or to pay any debts.

Long-term effects. These are the effects after your bankruptcy is completed. The fact that you now have a bankruptcy in your history will make it difficult for you to obtain credit. This will affect your ability to qualify for a mortgage, buy a car, or obtain a credit card. It is a long, gradual process to build up credit once you've declared bankruptcy.

It may also make it difficult for you to get a promotion or be given a position of trust at work, or to get hired by a new employer who does a credit check. You will probably also be starting over with fewer possessions than you had before your bankruptcy. Some of your property will probably get repossessed, and some of it may have to be sold. If a relative or friend co-signed a loan for you, that relative or friend will still be liable to repay the loan.

A bankruptcy may also cause you to lose your retirement benefits. Be sure to read section 8 of this book for more information on pension plans and how they are affected by bankruptcy.

You will have to be very careful not to get into debt problems again. You can only file for bankruptcy once every six years (refer back to page 11 of this book for discussion of this limitation).

EMOTIONAL
EFFECTS

In addition to the financial effects, most people experience some emotional effects when they file for bankruptcy.

Yourself. You may experience a feeling of failure or dishonesty. Failure because you couldn't manage your affairs better, or weren't smart enough to handle your money. Dishonest because you feel you are cheating your creditors. Although there are many logical arguments for not feeling this way, many people still can't overcome the feeling on an emotional level. The following categories are separate in some respects, but they are also part of how you see yourself. Regardless of how others really feel about your situation, you will see and interpret their reaction in terms of how you feel about yourself.

Your family and friends. If you are married, your spouse, and possibly your children, will have to know about the bankruptcy. You will need to prepare for how you will discuss it with them. You may also have to be prepared to deal with their feelings of failure, disappointment, and guilt. There may also be extended family members involved, such as parents, brothers, aunts and uncles, and friends. These people may or may not understand and sympathize with your situation.

Your employer. It is possible that you can keep your bankruptcy out of your workplace, but it isn't likely. Although your employer probably won't admit it, a bankruptcy may affect your ability to obtain promotions, or to be entrusted with certain responsibilities (such as handling money or accounts). Of course, the same thing may happen if you don't file, and a creditor files a wage garnishment.

For some, or all, of these reasons you should first explore whether you might avoid bankruptcy.

As you can see, there are some good reasons to avoid bankruptcy. There are also good reasons to file for bankruptcy, in the right circumstances. The remainder of this section will help you determine if the circumstances are right. First, we will look at your current income and expenses, then we will look at what you own and what you owe.

INCOME AND EXPENSE WORKSHEET (FORM 1)

In order to be considering bankruptcy, you must be in a situation where your income is not sufficient to cover your monthly expenses. To find out just how bad your situation is we will examine your current budget. Complete the INCOME AND EXPENSE WORKSHEET (Form 1 in appendix B of this book), according to the following guidelines:

- ☛ Be sure to use ***monthly*** amounts in completing this form.

- ☛ To convert a weekly amount, multiply the amount by 4.3.

- ☛ To convert a bi-weekly amount, divide by 2, then multiply the answer by 4.3.

The following relates to the INCOME portion of Form 1:

☛ Take Home Pay: This refers to your total pay after you deduct for taxes and social security. If you have other payroll deductions, such as for a medical or dental plan, uniforms, or savings plan, they should be listed under the EXPENSES section of this form. Therefore, add these deductions back to the take home pay shown on your paycheck. If your pay changes from paycheck to paycheck, obtain an average by dividing your yearly income by 12, or by some other appropriate method.

☛ Self Employment Income: Calculate an average monthly income if you are self-employed (either as your main job or as a second job). Consult a book that covers business bankruptcies, or see a lawyer, if you are self-employed and are incorporated, and have employees or a financially complex business operation.

☛ Interest and Dividends: This includes such things as interest on bank accounts, certificates of deposit (CDs), stocks, bonds, mutual funds, etc.

☛ Income from Real Estate: This is income from any rental property you own.

☛ Retirement Income: This includes pensions and other retirement payments from your prior employment.

☛ Alimony or Support Payments: This includes money you receive as alimony, maintenance, child support, etc. Only count these payments if you receive them on a fairly regular and dependable basis.

☛ Other: This might include such things as Social Security, unemployment compensation, disability benefits, welfare benefits, or income from loans you made to other people.

The following relates to the EXPENSES section of Form 1:

- ☞ Homeowners/Renter's Insurance: If homeowners insurance is included in your mortgage payment, it should not be listed here again. If you rent and have renters insurance on your possessions, you will be paying it separately from your rent payment, so list it here.

- ☞ Real Estate Taxes: If these are included in your mortgage payment, they should not be listed here again.

- ☞ Other Installment Loan Payments: This relates to all loans except your mortgage and auto loan payments. This will include such things as credit cards, home equity loans, boat loans, vacation loans, home improvement loans, and swimming pool loans.

The remaining items are self-explanatory. Just make sure everything is converted to a *monthly* amount.

Next, add all of your monthly income and write the total in the space for TOTAL MONTHLY INCOME. Add all of your monthly expenses and write the total in the space for TOTAL MONTHLY EXPENSES. Finally, subtract the total expenses from the total income and write the amount in the space for DEFICIT. This should give you a negative number, which will tell you how much money you are falling short by each month. (If you get a positive number, then you have either forgotten to list some of your expenses, or you are making enough money to meet your monthly expenses and should not be thinking about bankruptcy.)

PROPERTY WORKSHEET (FORM 2)

To put it simply, *property* is something you own (such as money, a house, a car, furniture, etc.), and a *debt* is money you owe. Property may also be referred to as an *asset*. The two things you will consider in trying to avoid bankruptcy are whether you can cut your expenses, and whether you can sell some assets and pay off some debts. First, it is necessary to explain the types of property and debts involved in a bankruptcy. Then, we will discuss some general guidelines for determining whether bankruptcy is right for you. Finally, we will discuss what can be done to try to avoid bankruptcy.

Property is divided into exempt and non-exempt categories. Remember, the purpose of bankruptcy is to help you start over financially. It would not be helpful to leave you without property, so the bankruptcy laws allow you to keep a certain amount of your property. The types and amounts of property you are allowed to keep are exempt property. The type and amount of property that is exempt is a matter of state law (and alternative federal law in some states). Although the Bankruptcy Code is a federal law, the question of exempt property is generally determined by your state government. Generally, most states exempt the following types of property, at least up to a certain value or amount:

- ☞ Motor vehicles.

- ☞ Clothing and personal effects.

- ☞ Household furnishings.

- ☞ Tools used in your trade or profession.

- ☞ Equity in a home.

- ☞ Life insurance.

- ☞ Public employee pensions. (See section 8 of this book.)

- ☞ Social Security, welfare, unemployment or workers' compensation, or other public benefits accumulated in a bank account.

Typical examples of non-exempt property are:

- ☞ The above items over a certain amount.

- ☞ A second car.

- ☞ A boat or recreational vehicle.

- ☞ A vacation home.

☞ Cash, bank accounts, certificates of deposit.

☞ Other investments, such as stocks, bonds, coin collections, etc.

The PROPERTY WORKSHEET (Form 2) which you will fill out next will divide your property into exempt and non-exempt categories. If you live in Arkansas, Connecticut, the District of Columbia, Hawaii, Massachusetts, Michigan, Minnesota, New Jersey, New Mexico, Pennsylvania, Rhode Island, South Carolina, Texas, Vermont, Washington, or Wisconsin, you have the following choices in determining what property is exempt:

1. Use the exemptions listed for your state **and** the Federal Non-Bankruptcy Exemptions, both of which are listed in appendix A of this book. (If you use your state exemptions, you may **not** use any of the Federal Bankruptcy Exemptions.)

2. Use the Federal Bankruptcy Exemptions **and** the Federal Non-bankruptcy Exemptions, both of which are listed in appendix A of this book. (If you use the Federal Bankruptcy Exemptions, you may **not** use any of your state exemptions.)

If you live in any other state, you may only use your state exemptions and the Federal Non-Bankruptcy Exemptions.

> **CAUTION:** Even if the property is exempt, you may still lose the property if it is tied to a secured debt. For example: Your home is exempt property under your state's laws. If you borrowed money from a bank to buy the house, and the bank holds a mortgage on the house, the bank can still foreclose and take your house if you don't pay.

The PROPERTY WORKSHEET (Form 2 in appendix B of this book) is divided into six columns, each of which have both a number and a title. The following instructions refer to each column by number.

In column (1), list all of your property. Do not list anything in more than one category. For each category of property in Form 2, check if any such items are exempt on your state's list in appendix A of this book. If so, be sure to list those items separately. For example, if your state exempts wedding rings, be sure to list your wedding rings as a separate item in the Jewelry category in Form 2. You should also compare your state's exemptions with the Federal Bankruptcy Exemptions at the beginning of appendix A, if you live in one of the states (listed above and in appendix A) which permit the Federal Bankruptcy Exemptions as an alternative to the state exemptions. Also Column (1) is divided into several categories of property, as follows:

☞ Real Estate: List any real estate you own, by each property's address or other brief description.

☞ Autos: Include cars, trucks, motorcycles, etc.

☞ Boats: Include boats, engines, boating equipment, as well as any other recreational vehicles.

☞ Cash on hand: This is cash in your pocket, wallet, purse, mattress, etc. It does not include money in a bank.

☞ Bank accounts: This is where you list all of your bank accounts, by your bank name and account number.

☞ Clothing: You can just give an estimate of the total value of your clothing. Only list specific items if they have great value (such as a mink coat, or original designer items).

☞ Jewelry: Costume jewelry need not be listed by item, but gold, diamonds and other precious metals and gems should be listed by each item.

☞ Household goods: This includes all of your furniture, pots and pans, dishes, personal items, etc. A general estimate can be given for most things. Although any items of great value should be listed separately, but first check to see it they fit in one of the other categories in this form.

☛ Collections: This is for such things as coins, stamps, paintings, books, and other valuable collectibles.

☛ Sports equipment: Include firearms, pool tables, golf clubs, etc.

☛ Business goods/Trade tools: This includes any such items you need in order to conduct your business or to engage in your occupation.

☛ Investments: This includes any stocks, bonds, patents, copyrights, licenses, etc.

☛ Insurance: This includes any cash value in life insurance policies, annuities, etc.

☛ Other property: This is where you list anything that doesn't fit into one of the other categories. Again, be sure to check your state's listing in appendix A.

Column (2) is titled VALUE. Fill in the approximate value of each of the items of property you listed under Column (1). For some items you will know the exact value, and for others you will have to make a good estimate. For such things as autos and boats you may be able to find a *blue book* (which may be any color) at your local library or at a local dealer, which will give approximate values. For other items, such as clothing, personal belongings and furniture, just estimate what you think you could sell these items for at a garage sale. Estimate low, but don't get ridiculous.

Column (3) is used to fill in how much money, if any, you still owe on any of the items listed under Column (1). For the purposes of this form, you only *owe* something if the item can be foreclosed on or repossessed if you fail to pay. For example, if you bought your dining set with your VISA card, it can't be repossessed. Therefore, you don't owe anything on the dining set. Next, subtract the amount owed in Column (3) from the value in Column (2), and write in the difference in Column (4). This will give you your equity in each piece of property. *Equity* is the amount of cash you would have if you sold the property and paid off the amount you owe.

For Column (5), refer to your state's listing in appendix A, where you will find a list of the items and amounts that are exempt. Also look at the beginning of appendix A to see if you are in a state that permits use of the Federal Bankruptcy Exemptions. If so, compare the state and Federal Bankruptcy Exemptions to see which would make more of your property exempt. The state exemptions will usually give you a better result, but not always. If you will get more exempt property under the Federal Bankruptcy Exemptions, use them instead of the state exemptions. For each item of property, you may find that item completely exempt, or only exempt to a certain value. The following examples will help illustrate this point:

☛ EXAMPLE 1: If you live in Florida, the home you live in (your *homestead*) is completely exempt, no matter what its value. If you have a home worth $100,000, it is fully exempt. This means you don't have to sell your house to pay off your creditors. (But if you have a mortgage, then you have to make your payments.)

☛ EXAMPLE 2: If you live in Illinois, only $7,500 of the value of your home is exempt. If your home is worth $100,000, you may only claim an exemption of $7,500. You would have to sell your home, or take out a new mortgage for $92,500 so that your equity is only $7,500. Of course you would have to pay your mortgage payments, if you could get a loan with your financial problems. Illinois does not allow the Federal Bankruptcy Exemptions, so you can only exempt the $7,500 allowed by Illinois.

☛ EXAMPLE 3: If you live in New Jersey, your home is not exempt at all. Whether your equity is $100,000 or $1.00, you would lose it in a bankruptcy if you use the New Jersey exemptions.. However, New Jersey allows you to use the alternative Federal Bankruptcy Exemptions, which would allow you to keep up to $15,000 in a home.

Look at your available exemptions in appendix A and determine what property is exempt. Fill in the amount of the exemption in Column (5).

In Column (6), place a check mark beside each item of property for which the debt is secured. (If necessary, re-read the part of this section on secured and unsecured debts.) If the debt for that property is secured, you will need to keep up your payment, or at least work out something with the creditor, in order to keep the property (even if the property is exempt in your state).

DEBT WORKSHEET (FORM 3)

DISCHARGEABLE AND NON-DISCHARGEABLE DEBTS

In a bankruptcy, debts are first divided into two types: *dischargeable* and *non-dischargeable*. A dischargeable debt is one that the bankruptcy laws allow you to discharge, or cancel. The best examples of dischargeable debts are the money you owe on credit cards, such as a Visa, Mastercard, or department store card, and medical bills. Most consumer debts are dischargeable in bankruptcy, and these are the types of debts that lead most people into a situation that requires them to file for bankruptcy.

If you have several credit cards, and you charge them all up to the limit, it is easy to get in over your head. It is easy to recall cases in which an individual, or more often a young couple, has charged as much as $15,000. And that was in addition to their mortgage payment and car payment!

A non-dischargeable debt is one that you will still owe after the bankruptcy is completed. Examples of non-dischargeable debts are:

☛ Student loans.

☛ Child support or alimony obligations.

☞ Delinquent taxes.

☞ Some court-ordered judgments.

☞ Debts arising from fraud (such as from providing false credit application information, from theft, or from obtaining credit with the intention of filing for bankruptcy to avoid payment).

SECURED AND UNSECURED DEBTS

Debts are also divided into two other categories: *secured* and *unsecured*. A secured debt is one that can be viewed as *attached* to a particular piece of property. The prime example of a secured debt is a mortgage. The mortgage means that, if you don't pay the money you borrowed to buy your house, the lender can take your house. Most car loans also include a *financing statement*, which is essentially the same as a mortgage. If you don't pay, the lender gets your car.

However, most credit card loans are unsecured. They are not tied to any particular piece of property. If you don't pay, the bank can't grab your property (at least not without going to all of the trouble of suing you and trying to attach your property later).

DEBT WORKSHEET (FORM 3)

Now, complete the DEBT WORKSHEET (Form 3 in appendix B of this book) according to the following guidelines.

This form is divided into six columns, five of which are numbered. The first column is to remind you of the types of property you have. In Column (1) list each debt by the lender's name and account number.

In Column (2) list what the loan was for, such as home, car, boat, vacation, etc. For your credit cards you don't need to list each little purchase you made, as the only purpose of this column is to help you remember what the loan is for, and to determine whether the loan is secured by any property.

In Column (3) write down the balance due on each loan. You don't need to have each one exact to the penny, but be as accurate as possible.

In Column (4) write in the same amount as Column (3) for each loan that is secured by a piece of property.

In Column (5) write in the same amount as Column (3) for each loan that is a dischargeable loan. For purposes of Form 3, a secured loan is not considered dischargeable, unless you are willing to give up that item of property.

GENERAL GUIDELINES

In order to determine whether you should file for bankruptcy, you need to evaluate your situation according to the following four factors:

1. Can you reduce your total monthly payments so that you can manage things on your income?

2. How much of your debt is dischargeable?

3. How much of your debt is secured by your property?

4. How much of your property is exempt?

Once you have done this, you can get a good idea of whether you can avoid bankruptcy and where things would stand after a bankruptcy. You will be able to estimate how much property you would be able to keep, and how much money you would still owe to creditors.

Let's look at your monthly budget first [refer to your completed INCOME AND EXPENSE WORKSHEET (Form 1)]. Examine each of your monthly expenses. Are there any that you can reduce or eliminate? Can you sell some of your property to pay off some of your debts? Can you move to a cheaper apartment, or sell your home and find an apartment that will reduce your monthly housing costs? Can you sell your late model car and buy a less expensive one? This is no time to think about maintaining your lifestyle. After all, it may be your lifestyle that got you into financial trouble in the first place! If you can make such adjustments to your expenses, you may be able to avoid bankruptcy. If such adjustments still won't help your situation, continue on to the next paragraph and look at the types of debts and property you have.

A general rule of thumb is that if you can discharge more than 50% of your debts, a Chapter 7 bankruptcy would probably improve your financial situation. To determine if your situation fits this guideline, refer to Form 3, take the total of Column (3) and divide it by 2. If the answer is equal to or less than the total of Column (5), you can probably benefit from a Chapter 7 bankruptcy. If the answer is greater than the total of Column (5), you may benefit from a Chapter 13 bankruptcy, or even avoid bankruptcy.

Be sure to read the next section on Alternatives to Bankruptcy. Following the instructions on planning a budget will help you to better understand your situation, even if you already know that you need to file for bankruptcy.

ALTERNATIVES TO BANKRUPTCY

If, after filling out Forms 1, 2 and 3 from appendix B of this book, it looks as if you may be able to avoid bankruptcy, this section will present some ideas for how you can get your debt problems under control. Of course, the first step is to *stop charging!*

CREDIT
COUNSELING

If you would like to totally avoid bankruptcy, you may want to see a credit counselor.

> **WARNING:** Beware of private *debt counselors* or offers for *debt consolidation* loans. Such "help" often only results in one large payment instead of many smaller payments, and you will still have trouble making that monthly payment. Furthermore, such operations charge counseling fees that only further take away needed cash. Soon you may be facing bankruptcy again. Also, *avoid* the now-famous *home equity loan.* This can end up converting your unsecured debts into secured debts, which means that you may not be able to file for bankruptcy without losing your home!

You can feel comfortable going to see a credit counselor who is associated with your local Consumer Credit Counseling Service. This organization can be found in the Yellow Pages telephone directory under the heading "Credit Counseling." This is a non-profit organization set up by creditors, such as banks, department stores, credit card companies and other businesses. A credit counselor will contact your creditors, help establish new payment arrangements, and help you set up a budget you can handle. However, if you miss payments on your new budget, you may still end up in a bankruptcy, and will have possibly paid hundreds of dollars to your creditors needlessly. In this situation, it would have been better for you to have filed for bankruptcy at the start.

A Consumer Credit Counseling (CCC) plan is similar to a Chapter 13 bankruptcy, but on a less formal basis. It is also cheaper, in that the cost of the CCC assistance is minimal (about $20.00), whereas higher court filing fees and other costs are involved in a Chapter 13 bankruptcy case. It will look better on a credit report to have a record of CCC assistance, than to have a record of a bankruptcy. The main financial difference is that a CCC plan will require you to pay your debts in full, whereas a Chapter 13 may only require payment of a portion of your debts.

If you feel a strong obligation to pay your creditors in full, you should consider paying a visit to your local Consumer Credit Counseling Service office.

BE YOUR OWN CREDIT COUNSELOR

In theory, there is nothing a credit counselor can do that you can't do. On a practical level, creditors are more inclined to listen to a credit counselor. Your creditors don't want you to file for bankruptcy, because it means they won't get paid in full. Because of this, they should have a strong incentive to be reasonable. Your main goal is to get the creditor to allow you to make smaller payments, over a longer period of time.

For example, George has a $1,500 balance on a credit card from a local department store. His payments are $74.89 a month, and the balance will take two years to pay off. If the department store will agree to accept payments over an additional year, George's monthly payment will be lowered to $54.23 a month. This lowers his monthly payment by $20.66. If he has ten loans like this, he could save over $200 per month, which may be enough to enable him to keep up his payments based on his income.

Planning a budget. The place to begin is by reviewing the INCOME AND EXPENSE WORKSHEET (Form 1), that you completed earlier. You will need this form and a calculator to plan your budget. (If you don't have a calculator or adding machine, you'll have to do the arithmetic by hand.) The copy of Form 1 you completed shows your budget as it is right now. Use a blank copy to start your new budget. Your total income will remain the same, so write it in under TOTAL MONTHLY INCOME. Enter this amount in your calculator. Now go through all of your expenses, and subtract each one from the TOTAL MONTHLY INCOME figure. First, identify the most important item, which is probably your rent or mortgage payment (unless you are prepared to go live with friends and relatives). Write this amount in the appropriate place on the form, and subtract it from your total income.

Next, identify your next most important expense, and so on. For each item, ask yourself if there is any way to reduce the amount you spend each month. If you can reduce the amount, then use the reduced amount, and subtract it from the total. Your essential payments are for housing (including utilities), food, and transportation (probably your car). In order to survive and earn a living, you need a place to live, food, and a way to get to and from work. If you are unable to make these essential payments with your income, or are unable to reduce these payments to that level, you may want to apply for some type of public assistance (yes, welfare) in addition to filing for a Chapter 7 bankruptcy.

Once you have subtracted the essential living expenses, you will be left with the total remaining income available to pay your creditors and other expenses. (Absolutely last on your list should be the "Recreation/Travel/Entertainment" expenses.) Now, start subtracting your payments for loans that are secured loans. These are any loans where your property can be repossessed if you don't pay. Most credit card debts are not secured by any particular property. The most common secured loans are for homes (including home equity loans), automobiles, boats, and occasionally furniture. If the only paper you signed was the typical charge card receipt for Visa, Mastercard, Sears, or other department store charges, the loan is not secured.

By now you are probably left with a small amount of income (if any at all), with which you can make payments on the rest of your loans. Add up the remaining loan payments, and subtract them from your remaining income. If your answer is -0- or more, then whatever adjustments you made to your expenses were enough to eliminate your debt problem. Now your only problem is to try to live according to your new budget.

If your answer is less than -0-, however, this is how much you need to reduce your monthly payments in order to avoid having to file for bankruptcy. Your next step is to try to persuade your creditors to adjust your payments to fit your remaining income.

Dealing with creditors. Your next task is to create a new payment plan to present to your unsecured creditors. What you need to come up with is a plan that is fair to all of your creditors. For your unsecured creditors, you will want to reduce each payment by a proportional amount. First, take the total monthly payments of your remaining debts, and divide it by the monthly shortage. This will give you the percentage you need to reduce each debt by in order to match your remaining income. For example, Sue has subtracted all of her essential expenses and secured loan payments from her income, and is left with $245.00. She has five monthly credit card payments as follows:

Visa	$150.00
Mastercard	65.00
Sears	50.00
Discover	23.00
Local department store	75.00
TOTAL PAYMENTS	$363.00

Sue's income is $118 short ($363 - 245 = 118). If she divides the amount she is short (118) by the total payments (363), she gets a figure of .325, which she will round up to .33 (or just about one-third). If she reduces each payment by .33 she will have enough income to meet the new payments. To find the amount to reduce each payment by, Sue will multiply each payment amount by .33, round off each answer, and then subtract this amount from each payment:

CREDITOR	OLD PAY	SUBTRACT	NEW PAY
Visa	$ 150.00	$50.00	$100.00
Mastercard	65.00	21.50	43.50
Sears	50.00	16.50	33.50
Discover	23.00	7.50	15.50
Local Dept. Store	75.00	25.00	50.00
TOTALS	363.00	120.50	242.50

As you can see, Sue has lowered her payments to fit her income, and has treated each creditor the same. If she can persuade these creditors to accept the lower payments, she has her new budget (and she has an extra $2.50 left over!). Of course this will increase the number of payments needed to pay off the loans.

Once you've worked out your new proposed payment amounts it is time to contact your creditors with your plan. Form 25 in appendix B of this book is a form letter you can use. Space is left at the top of the form for you to fill in the date and the name and address of the creditor. You will need to make a copy of this letter for each creditor. Just fill in the blanks according to your new payment plan, fill in your name and address (so it can be read), sign your name and mail a copy to each creditor. Be sure to type in your name, address and account number below your signature. It is a good idea to send these letters by certified, return-receipt mail. This will cost you a couple of dollars per letter, but you will later be able to prove the creditor received it if needed. Now sit back and wait for your creditors to answer. Be sure to fill in the return receipt number from the white receipt on both the green card and in the blank at the top of the letter (Form 25). You will note that the form letter states that your next payment will be according to the new schedule unless you hear from the creditor beforehand.

You may be asking, "Why should the creditor accept reduced payments?" If the creditor really believes you are serious about bankruptcy, and sees that you have a workable budget, he has every reason to accept your plan. His alternative is to let you declare bankruptcy, in which case he will receive absolutely nothing.

You should try to get your unsecured creditors to lower their payment requirements in order to fit your budget. Only after this fails should you contact your secured creditors about a new payment schedule. You may wonder why a secured creditor would agree to lower payments, when all he has to do is repossess or foreclose. Even a secured creditor would usually rather get paid than take back the property. It takes a lot of time and expense to repossess and resell property. And if you do file for bankruptcy it will take even more time and expense. A bankruptcy won't stop foreclosure or repossession, but it will delay it. Therefore, most lenders will work with you to try to avoid foreclosure, repossession, or bankruptcy. The key to success is showing the creditor a fair and reasonable payment plan that is clearly within your ability to maintain. If this doesn't work, you can still go to credit counseling, as discussed at the beginning of this section.

If this doesn't resolve your problem, you may need to proceed to the next section of this book to prepare for filing for bankruptcy.

Arranging Your Finances 4

> **WARNING:** *Use this section with extreme caution.* Before you file for bankruptcy, you may want to review your financial situation to see if there is anything you can rearrange to your advantage. Before we discuss various ideas, you need to be aware that you may be walking a fine line between acceptable practices and what the court might consider to be cheating your creditors. At a very minimum, you should not file for bankruptcy for at least 90 days after you make any of the changes discussed in this section, and if any changes involve a relative, you should not file for at least one year. However, each bankruptcy judge has his own ideas and attitudes, and some have determined that there was an intent to defraud where transfers were made more than a year before filing!

Now let's look at some things you might do before you file that will improve your situation after your bankruptcy is complete.

Incurring New Debts

If you will need to borrow more money to pay for necessities (such as for medical treatment, buying clothing for your family, or getting your car repaired so you can get to work), you may want to wait to file for bankruptcy until you have incurred these debts. This way, these debts can be included in your bankruptcy. A bankruptcy only affects those debts that you incur **before** you file. Any debts you incur **after** you file are not included in the bankruptcy. Just make sure you are incurring these new debts for necessary things, and not for "luxuries" (such as a vacation, a new stereo, or a night on the town).

SELL NON-EXEMPT PROPERTY AND BUY EXEMPT PROPERTY

The most obvious thing you might do is sell non-exempt property, and use the money to buy exempt property. For example, if you live in New York, furniture, a radio, TV, refrigerator, and clothing are exempt. However, a boat or second car is not exempt. Therefore, you may want to sell your boat or second car, and use the money you get to buy some furniture, a radio, TV, refrigerator, or some clothing. If you are like most people, furniture or clothing is probably your best bet, because you already have a radio, TV, and refrigerator. You will need to carefully read the list of exemptions for your state in appendix A of this book.

SELL NON-EXEMPT PROPERTY AND PAY CERTAIN DEBTS

Generally, you want to sell non-exempt property, and use the money to pay off either a non-dischargeable debt (such as a student loan or overdue taxes), or pay on a secured debt on exempt property (such as catching up that overdue mortgage payment).

☛ EXAMPLE 1: You have a non-exempt boat. You sell it and use the money to pay off a student loan. In the bankruptcy you would lose the boat anyway, so you may as well use it to reduce the number of payments you'll need to make after bankruptcy on your non-dischargeable student loan.

☛ EXAMPLE 2: You have a non-exempt second car. You sell it and use the money to pay off the balance of the loan for your primary car, which is exempt in your state. You get to keep your primary car after bankruptcy, and you will have one less payment to make (provided your primary car isn't worth more than the allowable exemption).

CAUTION: Be sure you don't pay off a loan on a non-exempt piece of property, because you will lose the property in bankruptcy anyway. EXAMPLE: You sell your second car and use the money to pay off your secured boat loan. The boat, being non-exempt property, is then taken by the trustee, to be sold and used to pay off other unsecured creditors. You have gained nothing.

You may also want to sell non-exempt property to pay off an unsecured loan. Paying an unsecured loan will only be of advantage under one or both of the following circumstances:

1. A friend or relative has co-signed the loan and you don't want to stick that friend or relative with having to pay the loan for you.

2. You want to maintain good relations with that particular creditor (such as your doctor or car repairman), and possibly be able to keep your ability to buy there on credit.

DEFRAUDING CREDITORS (DON'T!)

Rearranging your asset and debt situation can get you into trouble. If it appears to the court that you have made changes in order to cheat your creditors, the judge can let the trustee take and sell the new property you've bought, or he can even dismiss your case and not let you have a discharge of any debts. This will leave you in a much worse situation than you began.

In order to minimize the chances of problems, keep the following points in mind:

☞ Don't make so many sales that you would have enough money to pay off most or all of your debts (unless this is your goal in order to avoid bankruptcy). If you sell enough property to be able to pay off your debts, and don't pay them off, it will be considered fraud.

☞ Sell and buy property at market value prices. If you sell something for less than reasonable or market price, or buy something for more than it is worth, your creditors may object.

☞ Avoid sales to, or purchases from, relatives. If you decide this is absolutely necessary, be sure you make the exchange at market value.

☞ Don't sell something expensive and buy something cheap, planning to secretly pocket the cash. The judge or trustee can make you account for all of the cash you get from a sale, and either you come up with the extra cash or get your case dismissed.

☞ If the trustee, judge, or creditors ask you about your transactions before you filed, just tell the truth. One of the main things the court will consider in deciding if your action was fraud is your intention. Furthermore, if you are asked about a particular transaction, you can be sure that the person asking the questions already knows about it. Judges don't like people who lie or are sneaky (except other lawyers of course), so don't try to hide things. You are bound to get caught.

☞ Don't buy more non-exempt property on credit, then sell the items to buy exempt property. This is fraud.

☞ Don't go overboard and sell all of your non-exempt property. Leave something for the unsecured creditors so they don't feel cheated and challenge the transactions.

If all of this leaves you confused, and you want to take advantage of the things discussed in this section, you should consider consulting a lawyer.

GATHERING INFORMATION 5

Before you start preparing any forms, you will need to gather information about your finances. You should already have most, if not all, of the information you need. Your petition for bankruptcy will consist mostly of describing your financial situation at a certain point in time. You will need to gather all of your papers regarding your income, monthly expenses, assets and debts.

This information will be necessary for you to adequately fill out the forms to file for bankruptcy, and will also be useful in the event a judge, creditor or trustee asks you how you came up with the figures on your forms. The following comments regarding the type of information you need should answer any questions you have.

INCOME

For most people, income information will come from three primary sources: paystubs, tax returns, and W-2 statements. Your paystub should give the most current information. Look for a space that shows your "Year to Date," or "YTD" income. This will give your total earnings since the beginning of the current year. You can then count the number of weeks or months that have passed since January 1st, and divide that into your year to date earnings to get an average weekly or monthly amount.

If your paystub doesn't show a year to date figure, you can always add up the totals of all paystubs since the beginning of the year.

Another good source of income information is your previous year's income tax return, or W-2 statement. This information will be useable as long as you didn't get a raise, change jobs, or have any other change in income.

If you have additional income from such things as bank account interest, stock dividends, alimony, etc., get out any statements or other records that show this income.

If you have income from self-employment, you should gather your accounting records and tax returns.

EXPENSES

You should get out any papers or records that show how much your monthly expenses are. This should include at least the following:

HOUSING EXPENSE

If you have a mortgage, you probably have a payment book that shows your monthly payment. If not, look for cancelled checks to the mortgage holder, a copy of the note and mortgage showing the payment, an escrow statement showing the amount withheld each month for taxes and insurance, or some similar record. If you rent, you should have a copy of a lease that shows the monthly rent, or at least cancelled checks or receipts. If you can't find any of these, ask your mortgage company or landlord to send you a statement to verify the amount of your payment.

UTILITIES

Get out your monthly statements for your electric, gas, telephone, trash pick-up, and any other utility bill. Hopefully you've kept at least the last couple of bills. If not, be sure to keep the next one that comes. You could also write to the utility company and ask for a month-by-month statement for the past year (this information may be on some of your bills).

FOOD — This will not be as easy to find documentation for, since most people don't keep their sales receipts for food. However, if you normally write a check for your food shopping you can get an average from your checkbook information. If you can't find any such information, you probably still have a good idea of how much you spend on food for a week or month.

LOAN PAYMENTS — This information should be easy to find, in the form of a monthly statement or payment book. For credit cards you should get a monthly billing statement, which will give the balance owed and the minimum monthly payment. For other debts, such as auto loans, you will probably have a payment book.

OTHER DEBTS — This includes such things as insurance premiums, gas and maintenance expenses for your car, child day care, and any other expenses. Some of these items will have some sort of documentation and some you will simply have to estimate. This information should already be on the INCOME AND EXPENSE WORKSHEET (Form 1) you prepared earlier.

PROPERTY

Next, you need to make a list of everything you own. At this point we are not concerned with how much you owe, or what it is worth. Your list will include items such as the following:

REAL ESTATE — A deed or mortgage will sufficiently describe the property, by way of a legal description. You will probably only need the street address, but it's a good idea to have the legal description on hand.

VEHICLES — You will need the year, make and model of each vehicle you own. You probably already know this information, but it's a good idea to have some paperwork on hand, such as the title, bill of sale, registration, or loan papers.

BANK ACCOUNTS, ETC.

You will need copies of your most current statements, or other records, showing the current balance in all checking and savings accounts, certificates of deposit (CDs), IRA accounts, etc.

OTHER "FINANCIAL" ASSETS

This includes such things as stocks and bonds, mutual funds, annuities, life insurance policies with a cash value, and any kind of retirement account or fund. All of these things should have some kind of statement or other paperwork to show current values.

JEWELRY AND OTHER COLLECTIBLES

These items will probably not have any papers to document their value, unless you've had the item appraised or insured for a certain amount, or have borrowed money to buy the item. (Unless you still happen to have the receipt for an item that hasn't gone up in value much since you bought it.) When there is no documentation, make a list of the items and estimate what you could sell it for.

OTHER PERSONAL BELONGINGS

This category includes all of your furniture, clothing, pots, pans and dishes, and other everyday personal possessions. Of course, if any of these items are especially valuable, you need to treat them the same as jewelry and collectibles. Otherwise, just make a note in each category with an amount you think it would cost to replace the entire category. It is not necessary for you to list each piece of clothing, or each pot and pan, separately.

DEBTS

Your most likely debts are a mortgage, auto loan and credit cards. A debt will have an outstanding balance, and almost certainly an interest rate. This distinguishes a debt from other monthly obligations such as rent and utility payments. There will also be either a monthly statement or payment book, and probably some other paperwork you completed or received when you first obtained the credit. Mainly, you will need to know the name and address of whom the money is owed to, the account number, and the amount owed.

LEGAL RESEARCH

As the law is subject to change at any time, it is strongly suggested that you review your state's exemption laws before you file. The best place to do this is at a law library, and the best place to find such a library is at your local courthouse. Law schools also have good law libraries. There are two main sources of information: (1) your state's laws, which are named in your state's exemptions in appendix A of this book, and (2) the *Bankruptcy Reporter*, which is a nationwide collection of the decisions of the various bankruptcy courts. If you find an annotated set of laws for your state, they will also refer to significant court decisions.

STATE LAWS State laws are most often referred to as *statutes* or *codes*, and contain the exact law as passed by your state legislature. The laws are identified by numbers called *titles*, *chapters*, or *sections*, depending upon your state's system. A few states (namely Maryland, New York, and Texas) further complicate things by first breaking the laws down by subject, then breaking each subject down into sections. Once you find the particular law relating to your exemption, read the exact language to be sure there aren't any special qualifications required for the exemption.

In addition to the main volume, there is another place you should look. All of the states periodically update their statutes. Some states do this by a paperback supplement that slides into a pocket in the back of the hard-cover volume. Other states publish a separate hard-cover or paperback volume, which you can find as the last book of the series of laws. A few states have their statutes in loose-leaf binders, with separate supplement sections. Be sure to check the supplement.

Many states also have sets of laws that are *annotated*. This means that, after each law is stated, there is more information to help you understand what the law means. This includes brief summaries of court decisions interpreting that law. The supplements will also be annotated, which is where you will find the most recent information.

BANKRUPTCY
REPORTER

The *Bankruptcy Reporter* is a multi-volume set of books containing court decisions in bankruptcy cases. In most cases, you will only be concerned with the more recent, paperback volumes. The index in the front of each volume contains a summary of the court decisions. Look decisions from your state, which is abbreviated at the beginning of each summary.

PRACTICE
MANUALS

If you really want to study the details of bankruptcy law, look for a practice manual on bankruptcy. A practice manual is a book, or set of books, that gives detailed information on a specific area of law. A leading practice manual in the field of bankruptcy law is *Collier Bankruptcy Manual*, published by Matthew Bender, along with its companion *Collier Forms Manual*. Your law library will probably have a section devoted to such bankruptcy books. These books will contain additional forms, as well as detailed information on all aspects of bankruptcy law.

If you have any difficulty, ask the librarian for assistance. However, don't expect the librarian to give you any legal advice.

INTERNET
SOURCES

There are several sources of bankruptcy information on the internet. These include:

- ☞ Findlaw Bankruptcy:
  http://www.findlaw.com.01topics/03bankruptcy/index.html
  http://www.findlaw.com.01topics/03bankruptcy/gov%5Fflaws.html

- ☞ The text of the Bankruptcy Act may be founds at:
  http://www.law.cornell.edu/uscode/11/

- ☞ The text of the Bankruptcy Rules may be found at:
  gopher://hamilton1.house.gov/11d:uscode/title11A

- ☞ Notable bankruptcy court cases can be found at:
  http://www.usdoj.gov/ust/bankrpty.htm
  http://nacba.com/cases/index.htm

Other sources of bankruptcy information are:

- ☞ InterNet bankruptcy Library: http://bankrupt.com/
- ☞ ABI World: http://www.abiworld.org/
- ☞ Bankruptcy Alternatives: http://www.berkshire.net/~mkb/

COURT FORMS 6

UNDERSTANDING LEGAL FORMS

This section will help you to use and understand the legal forms that you prepare. These forms are found in appendix B of this book. Make copies of the forms you need, and save the originals from the book in case you make a mistake or need to make changes.

You will not need every form found in appendix B, as some of them will not apply to your situation. Certain forms apply only to Chapter 7 bankruptcies; certain forms apply only to Chapter 13 bankruptcies; and others can be used with either type of case. By now you should have decided upon whether you will file a Chapter 7 or a Chapter 13 case, so just follow the instructions in the next section of this book.

Legal forms are simply means of communicating necessary information to the court. Forms serve two main functions. First, they ask the court to do something (such as give you a discharge of your debts). Second, they provide the court with the information it needs to decide whether to give you what you ask for.

The following sections will tell you how to fill in each specific form. We will discuss how to fill in the top portion of the forms. You will notice that some of the forms begin as follows:

```
┌─────────────────────────────────────────────────────┐
│                                                       │
│           UNITED STATES BANKRUPTCY COURT              │
│                                                       │
│   _____ DISTRICT OF _____     │
│                                                       │
└─────────────────────────────────────────────────────┘
```

This is to show which court you are filing your papers with. Anyone who looks at your papers later will be able to know which court to go to in order to find more details about your bankruptcy case. Your creditors may need this information during the bankruptcy case. Also, after your case is completed, and you are applying for a mortgage or car loan, your prospective lender may need this information.

Each state has both state and federal courts. The first line tells you that this case is in the federal district bankruptcy court. Each state has at least one federal district bankruptcy court, and most have two or more. States that are divided into two districts will be divided one of the two following ways:

1. Eastern District and Western District.

2. Northern District and Southern District.

States that are divided into three districts will also be divided one of the two ways listed above, but will also have a Middle District. To find out which district you live in (and will file your case in), look in your phone directory for the number of the U.S. District Court or U.S. Bankruptcy Court. This should be listed in the government section of your phone directory. Call the court and ask which district covers your area.

The district designation will need to be typed in the first space on each form you use. If you live in a state with only one district, leave this space blank. The name of your state needs to be typed in the second space. For example, if you live in Florida, and you are in the Southern District, your forms will look like this when completed:

```
┌─────────────────────────────────────────────────────┐
│                                                       │
│           UNITED STATES BANKRUPTCY COURT              │
│                                                       │
│   ____Southern____ DISTRICT OF ____Florida____        │
│                                                       │
└─────────────────────────────────────────────────────┘
```

You may want to make a trip to your bankruptcy court clerk's office and ask to see a Chapter 7 or Chapter 13 case that someone else has filed. This may help you in completing your forms. The court records are open to the public, although you will not be allowed to take the case file out of the clerk's office. There will probably be an area at the clerk's office where you can sit down and review a file.

Except for the VOLUNTARY PETITION (which has its own instructions later in this book), the next part of the form looks like this:

In re _____   Case No._____

In the space after "In re," you will type in your name, as well as your spouse's name if you are married and filing together. The "Case No." will be left blank on your VOLUNTARY PETITION, because the court clerk will assign your case a number and fill it in this space when you file. Then, you will type in the case number on any papers you file later.

The forms in this book follow those approved by the bankruptcy courts throughout the country. The bankruptcy rules require all of the bankruptcy courts to accept these forms.

It is not absolutely necessary that you use a typewriter to fill in the forms, although typing is preferred by the court and gives a much more professional appearance than handwriting. If typing is not possible, then print the information and be sure that your writing can be easily read. The remainder of each form will be discussed in detail in the following section of this book. Just remember to complete the top part of each form.

Also note that many of the forms have two shaded circles at the top. The bankruptcy rules require all papers filed with the court clerk to be hole-punched so the clerk can insert them in a file folder. Get a paper punch and punch out the shaded circles.

The following subsections will give you detailed instructions for filling out the necessary bankruptcy court forms. (Forms 1 through 3 are the worksheets you completed in section 6. Forms 4 through 21, 24, 27, and

28 are the forms that you may need to file with the court.) Most of the forms are the same regardless of whether you have decided to file under Chapter 7 or under Chapter 13 of the Bankruptcy Code. For both Chapters you will file the following forms:

- VOLUNTARY PETITION (Form 4)

- SUMMARY OF SCHEDULES (Form 6)

- SCHEDULES A through J (Form 7 through Form 16)

- DECLARATION CONCERNING DEBTOR'S SCHEDULES (Form 17)

- STATEMENT OF FINANCIAL AFFAIRS (Form 18)

If you are filing under Chapter 7 you will also file a CHAPTER 7 INDIVIDUAL DEBTOR'S STATEMENT OF INTENTION (Form 19). If you are filing under Chapter 13 you will file a CHAPTER 13 PLAN (Form 20).

The following instructions relate to the form number, which is located in the upper outside corner of the first page of each form. Some of the forms are more than one page, and several have continuation pages for use if there isn't enough room on the first page.

VOLUNTARY PETITION (FORM 4)

To complete the VOLUNTARY PETITION (Form 4), first fill in the names, addresses and social security number in the boxes as indicated. Under the heading **VENUE** check the first box. (The second box is for businesses. If you have an affiliate, general partner, or partnership, you should consult a lawyer, or a business bankruptcy book.)

Under the heading **INFORMATION REGARDING DEBTOR**, check the appropriate box or boxes in each section. Under **TYPE OF DEBTOR** you should check either "Individual" or "Joint (Husband & Wife)," whichever applies to your situation. Under **NATURE OF DEBT** check "**Non-Business/Consumer**." Ignore sections A and B as they only apply to businesses. Under CHAPTER OR SECTION OF BANKRUPTCY CODE UNDER WHICH THE PETITION IS FILED check either the box for "Chapter 7" or for "Chapter 13," whichever one you've decided to use. Under FILING FEE check whichever box applies to your situation. Ignore the attorney information sections, and check the box for "Debtor is not represented by an attorney."

Under the section titled STATISTICAL ADMINISTRATIVE INFORMATION, simply check the appropriate boxes. This information can be determined from the information on Forms 1, 2, and 3 that you have completed. Note that the last two items only relate to Chapter 11 and 12 bankruptcies, so they don't apply to you.

At the top of the second page of the VOLUNTARY PETITION, type in your name. The case number will be filled in after you file the petition and get a number assigned by the clerk. The section headed FILING OF PLAN is only used if you have decided to file under Chapter 13 of the Bankruptcy Code. It is recommended that you file your Chapter 13 Plan with your petition. You will then check the first box in this section and type in the date you will be filing. If you can't file your plan with the petition, check the second box. The plan must be filed within 15 days of filing the petition, unless you are instructed differently by the court.

If you have filed for bankruptcy within the past 6 years, or if your spouse has filed a case that is currently pending, you will need to type in the information where indicated. Next, sign your name and type in the date under the heading INDIVIDUAL/JOINT DEBTOR(S). If you are filing a joint petition with your spouse, your spouse also needs to sign. If you are filing under Chapter 7 of the Bankruptcy Act, signatures are also required under the heading TO BE COMPLETED BY INDIVIDUAL CHAPTER 7 DEBTOR WITH PRIMARILY CONSUMER DEBTS.

You will note that Form 6 in appendix B is the SUMMARY OF SCHEDULES. Skip this form for now. It will be completed after you complete SCHEDULES A through J.

APPLICATION TO PAY FILING FEE IN INSTALLMENTS (FORM 5)

The APPLICATION TO PAY FILING FEE IN INSTALLMENTS (Form 5) is to be used if you are unable to pay the full filing fees at the time you file your VOLUNTARY PETITION. If you *are* able to pay the full filing fee when you file your VOLUNTARY PETITION, you can ignore Form 5. Call the court clerk's office and ask how much the filing fee will be. You can expect it to run about $175 (this is a filing fee of $130, plus an "administrative fee" of $45). At the time you file, you will still need to pay the $45 administrative fee and an additional amount to go toward the filing fee. You may pay the filing fee in installments, provided that there are no more than four installments and that the last payment is made no later than 120 days after the VOLUNTARY PETITION is filed. Complete the top portion of the form according to the instructions in "Understanding Legal Forms" at the beginning of this section. Then, fill in the installment payment terms on the lines provided in the form. Next, fill in the date and your address on the appropriate lines, and sign your name. This form will be filed with your VOLUNTARY PETITION.

If you don't think you can pay the fees in installments, ask the court clerk if there are any provisions or forms for having the fees waived entirely. Since 1994, several bankruptcy courts began testing this idea. The test period ends in October 1997, and it is not known what will happen afterward. The program could be discontinued, extended in the test districts, or expanded to other districts. The only way to find out is to ask the clerk. The test districts are: Illinois (Southern District), Montana, New York (Eastern District), Pennsylvania (Eastern District), Tennessee (Western District), and Utah. Your only other option is to contact a legal aid office in your area.

SCHEDULE A - REAL PROPERTY (FORM 7)

SCHEDULE A - REAL PROPERTY (Form 7) is where you will list all real estate you own. First of all, be sure to carefully read the instructions contained at the top of the form itself. This is the form where you list all of the real estate you own or have an interest in. In general, *real property* means land and things permanently attached to it. If you do not have an interest in any real property, simply write "None" in the first column that is headed **DESCRIPTION AND LOCATION OF PROPERTY**. If you do have an interest in real property, you will need to complete this form. In the first column, you will describe the property and tell where it is located. This does not have to be the formal legal description, but you should state the type of property (such as "home," "unimproved lot," "condominium," etc.), and the address, including the city, county and state. If you are renting the property, it should not be listed on this form, but should be listed on Form 13 instead.

In the second column, designated **NATURE OF DEBTOR'S INTEREST IN PROPERTY**, state the type of interest you have in the property. For most people who own a home, the ownership interest in the property is known as *fee simple*. The most common interests in real property are as follows:

☛ Fee Simple: This is where you own the property, with no obligation other than to pay the mortgage and taxes. You may own the property with someone else or by yourself.

☛ Life Estate: This is where you have the right to live in the property during your lifetime, but you can't sell or give it away during your lifetime, or leave it to anyone upon your death. This is commonly set up when the husband dies, and is usually done for tax purposes. He gives his widow a life estate so that she can live in the property until she dies, but then the property goes to their children.

☞ Future Interest: The most common example of this kind of interest is what the children have after a life estate for their mother. A person with a future interest will get the property someday, but only after some event occurs (such as the death of the person with the life estate).

One of these types of interests should be listed in the second column. If you own the property with another person who is not your husband or wife, you should also indicate the portion of the interest you own (such as "one-half fee simple," or "one-third future interest").

If you are not married, you may ignore the third column. If you are married, you need to indicate whether each piece of property is owned by the husband (H), the wife (W), both of you jointly (J), or both of you as *community property* (C). Community property only applies if you live in Arizona, California, Idaho, Louisiana, Nevada, New Mexico, Texas, Washington, or Wisconsin. Generally, this means that all the property either spouse obtains during the marriage is owned by both of them, and can be taken by the trustee even if they don't file for bankruptcy jointly. If you live in one of these states and are considering filing separately from your spouse, you should consult a bankruptcy lawyer.

In the fourth column, indicate the market value of the property. This is what the property could most likely be sold for. **Do *not*** take into account any money you owe on the mortgage. Be sure to total these amounts at the bottom of this column. In the fifth column, indicate the amount of money you owe on the mortgage or any liens on the property. If you do not owe any money on the property, write "None" in the fifth column.

Schedule B - Personal Property (Form 8)

On Schedule B - Personal Property (Form 8), you will list all of your property that is ***not*** real estate. Be sure to carefully read the instructions on the form itself. Also note that this form is several pages long. *Personal* *property* is all of your property that is ***not*** land or permanently attached to the land. This will be everything you listed in the PROPERTY WORKSHEET (Form 2), except for the real estate items. The types of personal property are listed in the first column of this form. Simply read each item and write down what you own in that category. If you don't own anything in a particular category, simply check the second column marked **NONE**.

> **CAUTION:** Be sure to list all of your property, even if you think it has no value. Otherwise, it may appear you are trying to hide property creditors, which could result in the dismissal of your case.

In the third column, marked **DESCRIPTION AND LOCATION OF PROPERTY**, describe each item in the category, and indicate where it is located by street address, city, county and state. If most of the property is at your home, you may write in "Unless otherwise indicated, all property is located at the debtor's residence." If you do this, be sure to indicate any property that is located somewhere else. Refer to appendix A of this book for the list of the exemptions for your state, and for the alternate Federal Bankruptcy Exemptions. Any item for which you may claim an exemption should be listed separately in this form. For example, item 11 relates to pension plans. If your state offers an exemption for a certain type of plan, be sure to indicate that your plan is of that type. (See section 8 of this book regarding pension plans.)

If you are not married you may ignore the fourth column. If you are married, you will need to indicate whether the property is owned by the husband (H), the wife (W), both of you jointly (J), or both of you as community property (C).

In the last column, indicate the market value of the property. Unless you know what the property is worth, you should use your best guess as to what it would sell for at a garage sale. You want to estimate on the low side, but don't get ridiculous or you may get challenged by the trustee or a creditor. Total the amounts in this column at the bottom of the third page of the form.

SCHEDULE C - PROPERTY CLAIMED AS EXEMPT (FORM 9)

The property you are claiming as exempt from your creditors must be listed in SCHEDULE C - PROPERTY CLAIMED AS EXEMPT (Form 9). First you need to check one of the boxes at the top, indicating whether you are using the Federal Bankruptcy Exemptions (the first box), or the exemptions for your state (the second box). Both types of federal exemptions, and your state's exemptions are found in appendix A of this book. The Federal Bankruptcy Exemptions are only available in certain states, which are listed under the federal exemptions in appendix A. If the Federal Bankruptcy Exemptions are available in your state, you need to compare them with those of your state to see which set will allow you to keep more of your property. If you select the state exemptions, you may also use the Federal Non-Bankruptcy Exemptions.

To complete SCHEDULE C - PROPERTY CLAIMED AS EXEMPT (Form 9), refer to Column (5) of the PROPERTY WORKSHEET (Form 2), where you have already identified the items you are claiming as exempt. You may want to refer once again to the information in appendix A of this book to be sure you are claiming everything to which you may be entitled. If you aren't sure whether you can claim an item, but it seems to fit on of the exemptions, then claim it! Let the trustee or a creditor question it. (Of course, don't claim something you know is not exempt, but if you genuinely aren't sure give yourself the benefit of the exemption.)

In the first column, write in a description of the property. Try to use the same categories as those for your state in appendix A. All of the property listed in this form should also be listed in either SCHEDULE A - REAL PROPERTY (Form 7) or in SCHEDULE B - PERSONAL PROPERTY (Form 8).

In the second column, indicate the statute or law that gives you the exemption you are claiming. Again, refer to appendix A of this book for the statute or law number. Examples of how to refer to these laws appear at the beginning of each state's listing in appendix A.

In the third column, marked **VALUE OF CLAIMED EXEMPTION**, state the amount of the exemption you are claiming. Be sure you are not exceeding the maximum amount of the exemption allowed as indicated in appendix A. For example, if your state only allows up to a $2,000 exemption for a car, don't show a $30,000 exemption for your Mercedes! In the last column indicate the full market value of the property.

SCHEDULE D - CREDITORS HOLDING SECURED CLAIMS (FORM 10)

Any secured creditors need to be listed on SCHEDULE D - CREDITORS HOLDING SECURED CLAIMS (Form 10). Be sure to carefully read the instructions at the beginning of the form itself. To complete this form refer to the DEBT WORKSHEET (Form 3), Column (4), which will show those creditors holding a security interest in your property. These will most likely be the mortgage on your home and any other real property, and the lenders on auto, boat or home improvement loans. (They are not likely to be credit card companies.) A creditor holding security is one who loaned you money to buy something, and has the right to take some of your property if you don't pay. This also includes anyone having a lien on your property, such as for work done on your home.

In the first column indicate the account number (if any), and the creditor's name and address. Place an "X" in the second column, marked **CODEBTOR**, if another person is also liable for the repayment of the debt. However, do not check this column if the other person is your spouse *and* you and your spouse have filed a joint bankruptcy petition.

If you are not married, ignore the third column. If you are married, then indicate here whether the debt is owed by the husband (H), the wife (W), both of you jointly (J), or both of you as a community property debt (C).

In the fourth column, first indicate the date the debt was created. Next, indicate the nature of the lien on the property. Refer to the first paragraph of instructions on the form itself for examples of the types of liens. If you aren't sure of the type of lien, simply write "nature uncertain" and ask the trustee later; or call the person or company you owe the money to and ask. Next, give a description of the property that is subject to the lien, and indicate the full value of the property in the space labeled VALUE $.

In the fifth, sixth, and seventh columns, indicate (by an "X") if the debt is *contingent*, *unliquidated*, or *disputed*. These concepts are very confusing, so don't hesitate to ask the trustee if you aren't sure. A contingent debt is one that will only be owed if some future event occurs (such as if a tax audit shows that a debt claimed by IRS is really owed). An unliquidated debt is one in which the exact amount hasn't been determined (such as where you know you owe a tax, but won't know the exact amount until you know the full amount of your income or expenses). A disputed debt is one you are contesting (someone is claiming you owe the debt, but you don't think you do or don't think you owe as much). If none of these apply, leave these columns blank.

In the eighth column, marked AMOUNT OF CLAIM WITHOUT DEDUCTING VALUE OF COLLATERAL, indicate the amount of the debt you owe. In the last column, indicate if any of the debt is unsecured (not attached to any piece of property). For example, if you owe $8,000 on your car, but the car is only worth $6,000, then $2,000 of the debt is unsecured.

Total the eighth column, and indicate at the bottom left if there are any continuation sheets attached. Note that there is a continuation sheet for this form. Indicate at the bottom left whether there are any continuation sheets attached. If you only use the first page, total the eighth column and type in the amount in the box marked Total. If you use one of more continuation pages, total the eighth column for each page and type the amount in the box marked Subtotal. Then add all of the subtotals and type the amount in the box marked Total on the last page.

SCHEDULE E - CREDITORS HOLDING UNSECURED PRIORITY CLAIMS (FORM 11)

Certain types of creditors have *priority*, which means that they will be paid from your non-exempt and non-secured property before other creditors. Most creditors with priority relate to the operation of a business, so they won't apply to most people filing for personal bankruptcy under Chapter 7 or 13. The priority claims, as listed on SCHEDULE E - CREDITORS HOLDING UNSECURED PRIORITY CLAIMS (Form 11), are as follows:

☞ Extensions of credit in an involuntary case. Since you are filing a voluntary petition, this does not apply to you.

☞ Wages, salaries and commissions. This relates to money that you would owe to your employee. If you have employees, you should either consult an attorney or a book that deals with business bankruptcy.

☞ Contributions to employee benefit plans. Again, if you have employees, you should consult a lawyer or a book dealing with business bankruptcy.

☞ Certain farmers and fishermen. This only applies to operators of grain or fish storage facilities.

☞ Deposits by individuals. This would apply to you only if you owe someone money for a deposit they gave you to purchase or rent real estate, goods, or services that you have not provided.

☞ Taxes and certain other debts owed to the government. If you owe taxes to the federal, state, or local government, you will need to check this box and list the debt.

Be sure to carefully read the instructions at the beginning of Form 11.

If you do not have any of these types of debts, check the first box on the first page of Form 11 that states: "Check this box if the debtor has no creditors holding unsecured priority claims to report on this Schedule E."

If you do have any of these types of debts, then check the appropriate box or boxes on the first page, and list the debt on the continuation sheet. Complete a separate continuation sheet for each type of debt listed. You will note that there is a space at the top of the continuation sheet for indicating the type of priority debt. To complete the remainder of the continuation sheet, follow the same directions for Form 10 (SCHEDULE D - CREDITORS HOLDING SECURED CLAIMS) given above. Be sure to total the amounts in the eighth column, and indicate at the bottom left how many continuations sheets are provided for SCHEDULE E.

SCHEDULE F - CREDITORS HOLDING UNSECURED NONPRIORITY CLAIMS (FORM 12)

All of the creditors not listed on any of the previous forms will be listed on SCHEDULE F - CREDITORS HOLDING UNSECURED NONPRIORITY CLAIMS (Form 12). In most cases this will be primarily credit cards, and other personal debts such as unpaid bills. Be sure to carefully read the instructions at the beginning of the form itself. This form also has a continuation sheet. You will note there is a box to check if you have no creditors to report on this form. If you have no creditors to report here, you need to go back to section 3 of this book and take another look at whether you can, or should, avoid bankruptcy. The main benefit of bankruptcy is getting rid of these unsecured nonpriority claims. If you have none to get rid of, you probably should not file for bankruptcy and may want to consult a lawyer or credit counselor.

Complete the first, second, and third columns according to the instructions for SCHEDULE D - CREDITORS HOLDING SECURED CLAIMS (Form 10), as indicated above.

In the fourth column, indicate the date the claim was incurred, the consideration for the claim, and any setoff you are claiming. For the "consideration," simply state what the debt was for, such as "student loan," "vacation loan," "dental bill," "car repair," "Visa," "Sears," etc. In some cases, a store may have required you to pledge some property as collateral in order to obtain the credit card. You should know if this is the case because you probably would have had to sign some additional papers instead of a simple credit card application. If this is the case with one of your credit cards, you should list it on SCHEDULE D (Form 10) instead of here. A *setoff* is a debt the creditor owes to you. For example, if you owe your landlord $800 in back rent, but he owes you $50 for plumbing repairs that you paid for, you have an setoff of $50.

Complete the remaining columns according to the instructions for the same columns in SCHEDULE D (Form 10), as indicated above. This form also has a continuation sheet, so be sure to indicate at the bottom the number of continuation sheets attached. Also, total the amounts in the last column.

SCHEDULE G - EXECUTORY CONTRACTS AND UNEXPIRED LEASES (FORM 13)

Any contracts or leases to which you are a party must be listed and described on SCHEDULE G - EXECUTORY CONTRACTS AND UNEXPIRED LEASES (Form 13). If you are not a party to any contracts or leases, simply check the box near the top of the form before the sentence "**Check this box if debtor has no executory contracts or unexpired leases.**" Be sure to carefully read the instructions at the beginning of the form itself.

In the first column, indicate the name and address of the other parties to the contract or lease. This includes anyone who is obligated the same as you, such as your apartment roommate if his or her name is also on the lease. It also includes the person to whom you are obligated, such as your landlord.

In the second column, describe the contract or lease. Examples of such descriptions are "apartment lease," "auto lease," "lawn maintenance contract," etc. In this column you must also list the nature of your interest, such as "lessee," "seller," or "purchaser." (If you are a landlord, you will state this as "lessor.") If you have a lease for nonresidential property, you need to indicate this; and if you are a party to a government contract, the contract number must be stated.

SCHEDULE H - CODEBTORS (FORM 14)

Anyone who is also obligated to pay all or part of any of your debts must be listed on SCHEDULE H - CODEBTORS (Form 14). You do not need to include your spouse if you are filing a joint bankruptcy petition. Be sure to carefully read the instructions at the beginning of the form itself. You will note there is a box to check if you have no codebtors. If you do have any codebtors, then indicate their name and address in the first column, and the creditor's name and address in the second column.

SCHEDULE I - CURRENT INCOME OF INDIVIDUAL DEBTOR(S) (FORM 15)

SCHEDULE I - CURRENT INCOME OF INDIVIDUAL DEBTOR(S) (Form 15) is where you list your income, and that of your spouse if you are married and are filing a joint petition for bankruptcy. You will also need to fill in your spouse's income if you are filing under Chapter 13, even if you are not filing a joint petition.

The top portion of this form asks form information about your family status and employment, and is self-explanatory. The lower part asks for a breakdown of your income and payroll deductions (and that of your spouse if you are married and filing a joint petition, or are married and filing under Chapter 13). All amounts should be converted to a monthly amount. The last sentence in the form asks you to describe any increase or decrease of more than 10% in any of the listed categories that you expect to occur within the year after filing the petition. Examples would be the termination of unemployment benefits, an anticipated layoff or wage reduction, or the loss of rental income from the imminent sale of the property.

SCHEDULE J - CURRENT EXPENDITURES OF INDIVIDUAL DEBTOR(S) (FORM 16)

The previous schedule listed your income. SCHEDULE J - CURRENT EXPENDITURES OF INDIVIDUAL DEBTOR(S) (Form 16) is to list your monthly expenses. Convert all amounts to monthly figures. If you and your spouse are filing a joint petition, but do not live together, you will need to check the box near the top of the form, and your spouse will also need to complete a separate SCHEDULE J (in which case you will need to make another copy of this form for your spouse to complete).

You will note that at the bottom of this form there is a section to be completed *only* if you are filing under Chapter 13 of the Bankruptcy Code. In item "A" use the total income figure from Form 15. In item "B" use the **TOTAL MONTHLY EXPENSES** from this form. Item "C" will give the total amount you have available to pay your creditors under your Chapter 13 Plan. If you are going to pay monthly, indicate "month" in item "D." If you are going to pay at some other interval, you will need to divide the figure in "C" by the appropriate number to indicate how much you will pay at each interval chosen.

SUMMARY OF SCHEDULES (FORM 6)

On the SUMMARY OF SCHEDULES (Form 6) you will give the totals from each of the schedules you have completed. Note that for each schedule you are to indicate the number of sheets used. You will need to count the number of continuation sheets for each schedule, and don't forget to count your spouse's separate SCHEDULE J - CURRENT EXPENDITURES

OF INDIVIDUAL DEBTOR(S) (Form 16) if appropriate. Be sure to add the totals of the columns where indicated. Do not leave any spaces blank. If there is no entry for an item, type "0" in the space for that item. Although you are completing this form after the other schedules, this form will come before the other schedules when you file your petition.

DECLARATIONS CONCERNING DEBTOR'S SCHEDULES (FORM 17)

By completing and signing the DECLARATIONS CONCERNING DEBTOR'S SCHEDULES (Form 17) you swear that your schedules are accurate to the best of your knowledge. To complete this form, type in the total number of sheets as indicated on the form, type in the date, and sign your name where indicated (your spouse must also do the same if you are filing jointly). Note the fine and jail penalties listed on the form for giving false information.

STATEMENT OF FINANCIAL AFFAIRS (FORM 18)

The STATEMENT OF FINANCIAL AFFAIRS (Form 18) is a lengthy form, but one that is not difficult to complete because the instructions on the form itself are rather clear. All you need to do is read each item and provide the information it asks for. For each item there is a box marked "None" to check if that item does not apply to you. Be sure you mark the "None" box instead of leaving an item unanswered. Some of the questions may require you to go back through your records for the past few years. Just answer the questions as best you can with the information you can recall or locate. Use additional sheets of paper if necessary, and be sure to indicate the number of the item being continued on the additional sheet.

Item 14 asks about property you have that belongs to someone else. This is to protect that person's property from your creditors. Of course, an easier way to deal with this situation is for you to return that property to the other person.

Note the instructions immediately before Item 16. You will not need to complete any more of the numbered items in this form (and can skip to the last page for your signature) unless you have been in one of the following positions within the past two years:

☛ An officer, director, or managing executive of a corporation.

☛ An owner of more than 5% of the voting stock of a corporation.

☛ A general partner in a partnership.

☛ A sole proprietor of a business, or otherwise self-employed.

Once you have completed all of the items you are required to complete, type in the date and sign your name where indicated on the last page of the STATEMENT OF FINANCIAL AFFAIRS (Form 18). Your spouse must also date and sign this form if you are filing a joint petition. Also, indicate the number of continuation sheets attached (type in "0" if there are none). Finally, note the fine and jail penalties listed at the end of the form for giving false information.

CHAPTER 7 INDIVIDUAL DEBTOR'S STATEMENT OF INTENTION (FORM 19)

If you are filing under Chapter 13 of the Bankruptcy Code, ignore this section and go on to the section about the CHAPTER 13 PLAN (Form 20). If you are filing under Chapter 7 you will need to complete the CHAPTER 7 INDIVIDUAL DEBTOR'S STATEMENT OF INTENTION (Form 20), which simply indicates what secured property you intend to give up to your creditors and which property you intend to keep. This form only applies to **secured** property.

In order to list an item under the part of this form designated "b. **Property to Be Retained**," you must either reaffirm the debt, redeem the property, or avoid the lien. Read the next paragraph, see section 8 of this book for detailed information on reaffirming debtors, redeeming property, and avoiding liens; then see a lawyer if you decide to list any property here.

You may also keep secured property by informally agreeing with the creditor that they will not foreclose or repossess as long as you maintain agreed upon payments. If you are current in your payments, you can probably keep the property by simply continuing your regular payments. This is the preferable situation. If you are going to proceed with such an informal arrangement, you will list the property under the part of Form 19 designated "**a. Property to Be Surrendered.**" This is because you are formally surrendering your rights under the Bankruptcy Code to reaffirm, redeem, or avoid the lien.

There can be many complications to reaffirming a debt, redeeming property, or avoiding a lien. Be sure to read more about these subjects in section 8 of this book. If you run into a situation where you are not certain that your creditor will not foreclose or repossess, and will allow you to continue payments, you should see a lawyer.

Date and sign the form at the bottom where indicated. This form is very poorly designed, however, it is the official form approved by the courts.

CHAPTER 13 PLAN (FORM 20)

If you are filing under Chapter 7 of the Bankruptcy Code, you should ignore this form. If you are filing under Chapter 13 you will need to complete the CHAPTER 13 PLAN (Form 20), which simply states how you intend to pay your creditor from your disposable income. At the bottom of SCHEDULE J - CURRENT EXPENDITURES OF INDIVIDUAL DEBTOR(S) (FORM 16), you will find your disposable, or *excess* income. This is the amount of money you have available to turn over to the trustee in order to pay your debts. The following instructions will help you complete your CHAPTER 13 PLAN (Form 20).

In the first paragraph, type in the amount and indicate the payment interval from the bottom of SCHEDULE J - CURRENT EXPENDITURES OF INDIVIDUAL DEBTORS (Form 16). In deciding the interval to use, you may want to make it the same as your paycheck schedule.

In paragraph 2, describe how you want to pay your secured debts. Remember, if you don't pay secured debts the lender can repossess the property. Therefore, you will want to keep up the full payments on these debts. List the name of the lender, the amount of the debt, and the periodic payment to be made.

In paragraph 3, describe how you want to pay your unsecured debts. First, deduct the total amount of your payments on your secured debts from your disposable income. This will give you how much is left to pay your unsecured creditors. Generally, you must pay each unsecured creditor the same percentage of the debt as the other unsecured creditors. This may be done over a period of up to three years. If you have enough income to pay all of these debts in full within three years, you will set up a schedule to accomplish this by dividing the amount owed to each creditor by 36 months. This will give you the amount to pay to each creditor each month. If you don't have enough income to pay all of your debts in full within three years, the following paragraph will help you determine how much you can pay.

To determine how much debt you can pay, use the following steps:

1. Take your monthly disposable income, subtract the total monthly payments to secured creditors, and multiply the answer by 36. This will give you the total amount you have available to pay over the three years.

2. Add total amount you owe to all of your unsecured creditors.

3. Divide the total from "2" above by the total in "1." This will give you the percentage of each debt you will be able to pay.

4. For each debt, multiply the total amount owed by the answer from "3."

5. Take the answer from "4" and divide it by 36. This will give you how much of your monthly disposable income should be applied to each debt. Convert this to match your pay period if necessary (such as to a weekly or semi-monthly amount).

In paragraph 3 of your CHAPTER 13 PLAN (Form 20), type in the name of each creditor, the amount to be paid each month, and percentage of the amount due that will be paid (from "3" above).

Paragraph 5 contains a box to check if there is an addendum to the form. This will be used if you need additional space, or if there are any special arrangements regarding the payment of your debts.

Date and sign the form. This form should be filed along with your petition, and *must* be filed no more than 15 days after filing your petition.

MAILING MATRIX (FORM 21)

The MAILING MATRIX (Form 21) is used by the clerk to make mailing labels in order to send notices to your creditors, and to you. On the MAILING MATRIX (Form 21), type in the following addresses (keep each address within a box): Type your name and address in the top left-hand box, then type in all of your creditors' names and addresses in alphabetical order in the other box, moving across the page from left to right. Check with the court clerk to find out if they have their own mailing matrix form, or any special requirements as to how they want it completed. Be sure to follow the clerk's instructions carefully. Also, include:

- ☞ Anyone who co-signed a loan.

- ☞ Anyone jointly liable for a debt.

- ☞ Your ex-spouse if you intend to discharge debts you assumed in the divorce.

- ☞ All creditors listed in the forms you just completed.

Do not include your spouse if you are filing jointly.

COURT PROCEDURES 7

FILING WITH THE COURT CLERK, ETC.

Once all of your papers have been prepared, you are ready to file them with the court clerk. This is not difficult, however, things will go smoother if you are organized and know what you can expect.

FINDING THE CLERK'S OFFICE By now you should have found out where the bankruptcy court is located. If not, the first place to check is the government listings in your local telephone directory. Look in the U.S. Government section for "Bankruptcy Court," "District Court," or "Clerk of the District Court." If this fails, there is probably a general U.S. government "information" listing that you can call to get the location and mailing address of the bankruptcy court clerk's office.

Only a few cities in each state have a federal court, so you may need to do some digging to find the one closest to you. If you are having trouble, try calling the law library at the county courthouse in your county, or try your local public library.

WHAT TO BRING The following checklists indicate what you should bring with you to the court clerk's office when you go to file your papers.

If you are filing for a Chapter 7 bankruptcy, you should bring:

- ❑ VOLUNTARY PETITION (Form 4)

- ❑ SUMMARY OF SCHEDULES (Form 6)

- ❑ SCHEDULE A through SCHEDULE J (Forms 7 through 16)

- ❑ DECLARATION CONCERNING DEBTOR'S SCHEDULES (Form 17)

- ❑ STATEMENT OF FINANCIAL AFFAIRS (Form 18)

- ❑ CHAPTER 7 INDIVIDUAL DEBTOR'S STATEMENT OF INTENTION (Form 19)

- ❑ MAILING MATRIX (Form 21)

- ❑ Check or money order for the filing fee.

- ❑ Note pad or paper, and pen, for writing down any information or instructions the court clerk may give you.

If you are filing for a Chapter 13 bankruptcy, you need to bring:

- ❑ VOLUNTARY PETITION (Form 4)

- ❑ SUMMARY OF SCHEDULES (Form 6)

- ❑ SCHEDULE A through SCHEDULE J (Forms 7 through 16)

- ❑ DECLARATION CONCERNING DEBTOR'S SCHEDULES (Form 17)

- ❑ STATEMENT OF FINANCIAL AFFAIRS (Form 18)

- ❑ CHAPTER 13 PLAN (Form 20)

- ❑ MAILING MATRIX (Form 21)

- ❑ Check or money order for the filing fee.

- ❑ Note pad or paper, and pen, for writing down any information or instructions the court clerk may give you.

Under either Chapter 7 or Chapter 13, you may also be filing an APPLICATION TO PAY FILING FEE IN INSTALLMENTS (Form 5), which needs to be filed with your other documents. If you are filing this document, your check or money order should be for the amount of the first payment listed on Form 5. For either type of bankruptcy, be sure you have at least the number of copies required by the clerk, plus a copy for yourself.

FILING   Although it is possible to file by mail, it is strongly advised that you go to the clerk's office and file in-person. It is easier to establish a friendly relationship in-person, and the more time you spend at the bankruptcy court the more comfortable you will feel with the entire process.

As you enter the clerk's office, look around for any signs that may help you figure out exactly where to go. There may be several windows, which may be marked for different purposes, such as "Filing," "Cashier," "File Check-out," etc. Go to the appropriate window, or to any window if you are uncertain, and tell the clerk "I'd like to file a Chapter 7," or "I'd like to file a Chapter 13."

The clerk will take your papers and examine them (or refer you to the proper window, where that clerk will take them). If everything looks in order, the clerk will then tell you how to go about paying the filing fee. Either that clerk will handle the payment, or you will be directed to the cashier's window. You will pay the filing fee, and receive a receipt. The clerk will also assign a case number, and will stamp or write the number on your papers. The case number should also be on your receipt. Your papers are now filed.

If the clerk determines that something is not correct with your papers, you will be told what is wrong. *Do not argue with the clerk.* The clerk controls your access to the bankruptcy system, and you don't want to make an enemy of the clerk. Clerks cannot give you legal advice, but they will usually tell you what is wrong with your papers, and give you some idea of how you can fix the problem. The kind of problem the clerk will identify is one of form, such as you forgot to sign something, forgot to fill in a space, need another type of form, need to submit an extra copy, etc. All you can do is find out what the clerk wants, then do it. You may be able to correct the problem at the clerk's office.

If you try to satisfy the clerk, but are still getting your papers rejected or don't understand what is required, you may want to consult a lawyer. You can also politely tell the clerk that you aren't understanding the problem, and ask him or her to explain it again, or have another clerk try to explain it to you. Although most clerks are pleasant, helpful people, you sometimes run into a simply nasty clerk. You must still be polite, and try to win over the clerk; but if this doesn't work there is nothing wrong with asking for the clerk's supervisor. Just don't get angry under any circumstances. Remain calm and polite.

STOP MAKING
PAYMENTS

If you haven't already stopped making payments, you should stop once your petition is filed (except for payments on any secured debts if you want to keep the property). From this point on, all payments for anything must be approved by the trustee. It's all right to buy food, gas for your car so you can get to work, and to pay for any necessary medical expenses, but that's about all. It will take awhile to have a trustee appointed, but as soon as you receive a notice in the mail with the name of the trustee, contact the trustee as soon as possible. Tell the trustee that you just wanted to make an initial contact, and ask him or her if it is all right to pay any bills you feel you need to pay. Also ask the trustee any other questions you have. If you are continuing to make payments on secured property (such as your mortgage or car payment), mention this to the trustee.

Filing your petition operates as an *automatic stay*, which prohibits your creditors from taking any collection action, or from cutting off any services to you. Once your petition is filed, you may want to be sure to get your creditors off your back by sending them a letter notifying them that you have filed. Form 22, found in appendix B of this book, is a form letter for this purpose. Space is left at the top for the date and the creditor's address. Sign your name at the bottom, and below your name, type in your name, address, and account number. If you have a particularly bothersome creditor, you may want to send the letter by certified, return-receipt mail. Let the trustee know if any creditors continue to bother you.

CREDITORS' MEETING

After you have filed your case, the clerk will do several things. Using the MAILING MATRIX (Form 21) you provided and the information in your supporting documents, the clerk will send a notice to all of your creditors telling them that you have filed for bankruptcy. A trustee will also be appointed to your case, who will then schedule a meeting of creditors. Copies of any documents issued by the clerk or the trustee will be sent to you. Read them carefully, and call the clerk's office if you don't understand them. Most of these papers will not require you to do anything, but some may require some type of response.

You may also receive copies of any papers your creditors may file with the clerk. Again, these don't require you to do anything, but keep copies anyway.

You will receive a notice of the date, time and place of the meeting of creditors, which you must attend. The nature of this meeting varies slightly depending upon whether you selected a Chapter 7 or a Chapter 13 proceeding.

CHAPTER 7 CASES
In a large number of cases no creditors come to the meeting. The trustee will review your papers and ask you some questions. The questions are usually to verify what is in your papers, or to fill in information that you may have left out.

A few days before the meeting, call the trustee and ask him or her to tell you what information you should bring to the creditors meeting. In all cases, be sure to bring copies of all the papers you filed and all the papers you have received regarding your case. You should also bring tax returns and other documents that support the information in the papers you filed. Each court may have its own particular requirements, which is why it is a good idea to ask the trustee.

If creditors do attend the meeting, they also have the right to ask you questions. A creditor's usual concern is whether you have identified all of your non-exempt property, and whether such property has been turned over to the trustee for sale. Answer all of the questions honestly, as you will be under oath.

If the trustee decides that your any non-exempt property is not worth enough to justify trying to sell it, he or she may *abandon* the property. This means that you will get to keep it, even though it is not exempt.

CHAPTER 13 CASES
Creditors are more likely to attend the meeting in a Chapter 13 case than in a Chapter 7 case. They are concerned about getting the most out of your proposed payment plan. They will ask questions about the reasonableness of your payment plan, and the likelihood that you will be able to carry it out. The trustee will also ask some questions. Again, you are under oath, so answer honestly.

If the creditors and the trustee approve of your plan, it will be accepted by the court. If the plan is not approved, you may either negotiate changes in the plan to make it acceptable, stick to your plan and let the judge decide if it is acceptable, or convert your case to a Chapter 7 bankruptcy. To convert your case, see section 8 of this book.

Once your plan is approved, the trustee will probably order that the payments be deducted directly from your paycheck by your employer. This amount will be sent to the trustee, who will make the required payments to the individual creditors.

Until the paycheck deduction goes into effect, however, you are responsible for making certain that the payments are made. Unless the court orders something different, payments must begin 30 days after you file your plan with the court. This may be before the creditors meeting, in which case you should still begin your payments. If your plan ends up not being approved, the creditors will be required to refund any payments you have made.

COURT HEARING AND DISCHARGE

Depending upon the procedures in your particular bankruptcy court, you may or may not have to appear before the judge. If the trustee determines that everything is in order, you may receive a discharge without having to attend a hearing.

CHAPTER 7
CASES

In a Chapter 7 bankruptcy, once you have done all that is required to settle the case (turned over your non-exempt assets to the trustee, paid the filing fee and any other costs required, etc.) an order will be entered discharging all of your dischargeable debts. As has already been discussed, you will not be discharged from the following types of debts:

☞ Taxes, fines, or penalties owed to the government.

☞ Alimony or child support.

☞ Certain types of student loans.

☞ Obligations as a result of criminal or fraudulent actions.

☞ Any debts which were not declared in your bankruptcy, or which involve creditors not timely notified.

CHAPTER 13
CASES

In a Chapter 13 case, you will be entitled to a discharge once you have completed all of the payments required by your payment plan. This is more likely to require a brief court hearing with the judge.

ALL CASES

In either case, the judge will probably only talk to you about the effects of the bankruptcy discharge; caution you to avoid getting in debt again; possibly ask a few questions to assure himself that everything has been done properly; and make sure that you understand the meaning of the discharge. Your particular bankruptcy court may even have mass discharge hearings, in which many debtors are discharged at the same time and no questions are asked. All the judge does is give everyone a brief lecture about how your debts are now discharged, and how you should avoid getting into financial trouble again.

SPECIAL CIRCUMSTANCES **8**

This section will discuss several matters that do not apply to most simple bankruptcy cases. If any of these situations apply to your case, you may want to discuss them with a lawyer. Of course you should take a look at how much you may save, in contrast to how much a lawyer may cost you. The first two items mentioned have forms in appendix B of this book, and you can probably do them without an attorney. However, the other items will often require an attorney's assistance.

AMENDING YOUR PAPERWORK

If, after you file your VOLUNTARY PETITION (Form 4) and other papers, you discover that you have made an error, you may amend whatever papers are necessary to correct the error. This will involve completing the AMENDMENT COVER SHEET (Form 27), as well as whatever forms you need to amend. Some courts will require you to fully complete the new form, while others will allow you to simply note the item being changed. You will need to call the court clerk to find out which you need to do. At the same time, ask the clerk if there is any filing fee for the amended form.

To complete the AMENDMENT COVER SHEET (Form 27), after the first sentence, type in the name of the form or forms you are amending. Be sure to also complete the top portion of the form, as well as the date and signature portions at the bottom. Then attach the amended forms containing the new or changed information. You need to be sure to check whether the new information on one form also requires new information on other forms, and to include all forms that need changing. Also, certain changes may mean that you need to re-notify creditors, especially if the creditors' meeting has already been held. Check with the trustee or clerk to see if you need to re-notify all of your creditors. If you do, you will need to send a copy of your AMENDMENT COVER SHEET and the changed documents to each creditor, and will need to complete a CERTIFICATE OF MAILING (Form 24). To complete Form 24 fill in the title of the documents you send, and the name and address of all the creditors or others you send copies to. If the creditors' meeting has already been held, another meeting may need to be scheduled.

CHANGING FROM CHAPTER 13 TO CHAPTER 7

If you filed your case under Chapter 13 of the bankruptcy act, and have determined that you need to convert your case to Chapter 7, you need to complete a MOTION TO CONVERT TO CHAPTER 7 (Form 28). This form only requires you to complete the top portion and the date and signature portion. At the time you file this form, also include any other forms needed for a Chapter 7 bankruptcy as described in section 6 of this book [usually only the CHAPTER 7 INDIVIDUAL DEBTOR'S STATEMENT OF INTENTION (Form 19).]

LIEN AVOIDANCE

Lien avoidance is a procedure that allows a debtor to keep certain property that might otherwise be subject to repossession. Before reading about this any further, you should know that this is not available if you live in the following states: Kentucky, Louisiana, Maryland, Mississippi,

Tennessee, and Utah. Also, it is only available in Connecticut, Texas, and Washington if you use the Federal Bankruptcy Exemptions. With the possible exception of Connecticut, it is most likely that you will find the state exemptions more of an advantage in these states, especially if you own a home. Furthermore, lien avoidance only applies to exempt property, and you can't avoid more than the exemption allows.

Next, you need to see if you have either of the two types of liens to which this can apply: (1) those created by a court judgment, and (2) those created when you used property you already had as security for a new loan. You may not avoid a lien if you took out the loan in order to buy the secured piece of property. Therefore, if you have no court judgments, and your secured debts all relate to the items you purchased, you are not eligible for lien avoidance.

There are three other important limitations on the use of lien avoidance. First, you can't avoid a lien on your vehicle, unless it is used as a part of your business (which does not include use to get to and from work). Second, if the lien is for more than the exemption amount for that item, the lien will only be reduced and the creditor may still repossess if the amount remaining isn't paid immediately. Third, lien avoidance can only be accomplished by filing more papers with the court, possibly leading to a court battle with the creditor, and even the necessity for an appraisal of the property.

REDEMPTION

Redemption is where you agree to pay the creditor a lump sum, based upon the market value of a piece of exempt property. This is generally only advisable if the property is worth less than the amount owed on the loan. Instead of paying off the full loan, you only pay the amount the property is worth. This is done because if the creditor repossesses the property, he will only be able to sell it for the market value as the remainder of the loan is discharged in the bankruptcy.

However, there are limitations here also. First, three conditions must be met: (1) the debt must be a consumer debt, meaning it is for personal use, as opposed to business use, (2) it must be for tangible, personal property (as opposed to items like stocks and bonds), and (3) you must be claiming the property as exempt, or the trustee must abandon the property (which is usually done because the property is of little value).

REAFFIRMING A DEBT

Reaffirming a debt (also called *reaffirmation*) is where you and your creditor agree that the debt will still be owed after the bankruptcy and that you will continue to make payments. This requires a written agreement, signed by you and your creditor, and must contain certain provisions. A preferable alternative to this is for you to bring your payments current before filing for bankruptcy, and keep up your payments so the loan is not in default. Reaffirmation should be a last resort, as it takes negotiating with the creditor, leaves you still liable for a debt, and requires the preparation of a written legal agreement. Economically, reaffirmation often only makes sense if the loan is not current, you owe considerably less money than the property is worth, and the property is exempt.

LAWSUITS

If you are involved in a lawsuit in which anyone is suing for money (such as a lawsuit for personal injuries or to collect a debt), to foreclose or repossess your property, or to evict you from your residence, you need to immediately notify the court and the creditor that you have filed for bankruptcy. This will bring the lawsuit to a dead stop, and your creditor will have to get the bankruptcy court judge's permission to continue with the lawsuit. The formal way to do this is to file a form called a SUGGESTION OF BANKRUPTCY (Form 23), with the court where the lawsuit is pending. *Do not* file this form in the bankruptcy court. You will need to complete the top portion of the form in exactly the same manner as your other court papers in the lawsuit read (*not* the way the bankruptcy papers read), and file it with the clerk of that court (*not* the bankruptcy clerk).

PENSIONS AND RETIREMENT PLANS

The question here is whether you can keep your pension plan as exempt property. As you are about to see, this can get very complicated, so you would be wise to consult a bankruptcy attorney, especially if you have a sizable pension plan that you are relying upon to see you through retirement. First you need to determine if your pension plan is an *ERISA-qualified* plan. You can find this out by asking your employer's pension plan administrator. Such plans are covered by the Employee Retirement Income Security Act (or *ERISA* for short).

The United States Supreme Court has caused a great deal of confusion over whether an ERISA-qualified plan is exempt, although it now appears to have straightened things out. This confusion began in 1990, when the Supreme Court said that states cannot exempt ERISA-qualified pension plans, because only the U.S. government can pass laws concerning such plans. It then became a complicated matter to decide if you could exempt your ERISA-qualified benefits. This involved determining whether your state would allow you to use the Federal Non-Bankruptcy Exemptions, whether certain other complicated conditions existed, and whether you should do this considering your other exempt property. If you did not live in one of the states allowing the Federal Non-Bankruptcy Exemptions, bankruptcy courts in certain other states had decided that ERISA-qualified benefits were not a part of the bankruptcy estate. At that point it seemed that the only safe bet was to consult an attorney to find out what you had to do in your state.

Fortunately, in June of 1992, the United States Supreme Court issued a new ruling that ERISA-qualified pension plans are exempt from creditors by the ERISA law itself. Therefore, if you have an ERISA-qualified plan, claim it as exempt on SCHEDULE C - PROPERTY CLAIMED AS EXEMPT (Form 9). In the second column, headed SPECIFY LAW PROVIDING EACH EXEMPTION, type in: "11 U.S.C. §541(c)(2); 29 U.S.C. §1056(d)(1); and *Patterson v. Shumate*, 112 S.Ct. 2242 (1992)." These are the references to the federal law and the Supreme Court opinion making ERISA-qualified plans exempt. If your state also has a law exempting ERISA-qualified plans (see your state's listing in appendix A), type in the reference to that law also.

If you do not have an ERISA-qualified plan, you need to see if your state exemptions cover your plan. If your plan is not covered by a state exemption, you may want to find out if you can cash in your pension. You can then use the money to buy exempt property (but be sure to read Section 4 of this book before you try this).

PENSIONS AND
DIVORCE

If you were divorced, your pension plan benefits may have been divided between you and your ex-spouse. If your plan is not exempt, whether your ex-spouse still gets his or her share may depend upon how the plan was divided in the divorce case. If the plan was divided by a *Qualified Domestic Relations Order* (or QDRO, which is pronounced "quadro" by lawyers), your ex-spouse will still receive their share. However, if the court simply ordered you to pay your ex-spouse their share, you may be able to discharge this debt to your ex-spouse in bankruptcy. If you want to do this, you need to consult a bankruptcy lawyer.

AFTER YOUR DISCHARGE 9

Once you receive your discharge, you need to think about the future. The two main things you need to do are make sure that you don't get into financial trouble again, and start building credit again.

HANDLING YOUR FINANCES

From the INCOME AND EXPENSE WORKSHEET (Form 1) you have an idea of how to prepare a budget. Use the MONTHLY BUDGET (Form 26) is a MONTHLY BUDGET to help keep your financial matters under control. Make additional copies of Form 26 to use in the months ahead. Your budgeting has three main goals:

1. Assuring that you aren't spending more than you earn.

2. Assuring that you will have the money available when the bill is due.

3. Developing a savings plan.

First of all, you should have a checking account if you don't already. Shop around for a bank with the lowest minimum balance for free checking, or the lowest checking charges. If you are eligible to join a credit union, you will probably find they have the best deal around.

There are dozens of different checking account arrangements, so compare. Use the top line of the first column of the MONTHLY BUDGET (Form 26) to write in the total amount in your checking account. Your job is to decide which of the debts listed needs to be paid before your next paycheck, and how much of the total needs to be assigned to each of those debts. Use the other columns to allocate your next several paychecks to your debts. Hopefully, after deducting all of the debt payments from the amounts in the top column, something will be left over.

Ideally, experts say, you should save approximately 10% of each paycheck. For many people this seems impossible. But that is no excuse for not trying to save something. If you have never saved, try it for awhile. You may be surprised to find out that the feeling you get from looking at a bank account balance with an emergency cushion of $200 or $1,000 is as good as the feeling you'd get from spending that money.

The important thing is not to buy something unless you know exactly where you will get the money to pay for it when the bill is due. Whenever you think about buying on credit, look at your budget and ask yourself where the money will come from. It certainly can't come from the rent money, or from the food money. It should only come from the "Spending" money, such as from next week's paycheck. If so, then subtract that amount from the "Spending" line in the column for next week's check, and write it on one of the lines for "Credit Payments," also writing in the name of the store or other credit card involved.

OBTAINING CREDIT (IF YOU DARE!)

One of the problems, or maybe it's a blessing in disguise, of going through a bankruptcy is that it will be difficult to obtain credit. During the bankruptcy you "enjoyed" finding out what life is like without the use of credit, and it's a good idea to do without credit until you are sure that you can keep your finances under control. However, in our society, credit is almost essential if one is to improve one's standard of living.

Buying a home is frequently a better deal than renting one. Also, some essential items, such as cars, are very difficult to pay for in cash. So it is a good idea to begin establishing some credit once you have things (including your spending habits) under control.

LOCAL STORE CREDIT CARDS

One way to begin is to apply for a credit card from a local store. Almost every type of store now has its own credit cards, particularly local department stores and hardware stores. Many of these stores will issue a temporary card immediately upon filling out an application. Go into the store, fill out the application (which usually only asks your name, address and where you work), then buy something immediately with the temporary card. Even if the application is later rejected, you still have an obligation to make the payments on the item you bought, and that repayment will be something positive in your new credit record. You can always do the same thing the next time you need to buy something at that store. Eventually, your timely payment will be noticed and you will get an application for a permanent card approved.

MAJOR CREDIT CARDS

Until you get a few local cards, and establish a payment record on each, you should avoid applying for a major card (such as VISA or Mastercard), and avoid applying for a card at a major, nationwide department store (such as Sears or J.C Penney). Such applications will almost certainly be rejected.

BORROWING FROM YOUR BANK

Another way to establish credit is to borrow against your own money. If you can accumulate some money in a savings account, the bank will probably allow you to borrow money against the savings account. Once you pay back the money, you've taken the first step toward establishing a positive credit history. You will have to pay a little interest, but the object here is to establish credit, not make a brilliant deal. For example, say you have $500 in a savings account. Borrow $250 against the account for a period of 30 days. Take the $250 and put it in your checking account. At the end of the 30 days, write a check to pay off the loan (even at an annual interest rate of 22%, this will mean writing a check for about $254.59). You will be paying $4.59 interest for the privilege of establishing some credit, which is not very expensive.

APPENDIX A
EXEMPTIONS (FEDERAL AND STATE-BY-STATE)

This appendix is used to find what exemptions are available to you. In addition to listing the exemptions available in each state, the federal exemptions are also listed. There are two types of federal exemptions, one is called "Federal Bankruptcy Exemptions" and the other is called "Federal Non-Bankruptcy Exemptions." The Federal Bankruptcy Exemptions are not available in all states, so check the list at the beginning of the Federal Bankruptcy Exemption listing. If the Federal Bankruptcy Exemptions are allowed in your state, you will need to choose between the state exemptions and the Federal Bankruptcy Exemptions. You will need to compare the state exemptions to the Federal Bankruptcy Exemptions to determine which way will allow you to keep more property. In most cases the state exemptions will be better for you, but make the comparison just to be sure. The Federal Non-Bankruptcy Exemptions are available along with your state's exemptions.

Under the listing for each state you will find a notation as to whether the Federal Bankruptcy Exemptions may be used. Under the heading MISCELLANEOUS, there is also a reminder for you to use any of the Federal Non-Bankruptcy Exemptions that may apply to you.

The following listings give the section number for the applicable state law, and the exemption that relates to that section. At the beginning of each state's section, you will find information (with an example in parentheses) about how to write the statute reference in the second column of Schedule C. If no amount is stated, the amount of that type of property you may claim is unlimited. Where an amount is stated, you may only claim up to that amount as exempt. If you want to be sure you understand the exemption, go to your library and look up the actual language in that section of your state's law. Many states' law books have volume numbers on them. Where applicable, advice is given to ignore the volume number because it is not part of the official manner of referring to the law in your state. Refer to section 9 of this book for more information about statutes and legal research.

Doubling Exemptions. Some states allow a husband and wife to each claim a separate exemption. For example, if an automobile is exempt up to $3,000 in equity, the husband and wife may each claim an auto up to $3,000. This is referred to as *doubling* the exemption. An asterisk (*) after an item indicates that doubling is specifically prohibited by law. Two asterisks (**) indicates that doubling is specifically approved by law. No notation indicates that the law does not state whether doubling is permitted, so you may want to list the exemption for both husband and wife, and see if the trustee accepts it.

Note Concerning "ERISA" Pension Benefits. These are benefits from retirement plans which qualify under the federal Employee Retirement Income Security Act ("ERISA" for short). Your employer or retirement plan administrator can tell you whether your plan is an ERISA-qualified plan. Most states have laws providing for a bankruptcy exemption for ERISA-qualified retirement plan benefits. Whether the states can exempt such plans has been the source of much dispute in past years. The Supreme Court has said that ERISA-qualified pension plans may be exempted by the states. You should check with a bankruptcy lawyer if you run into any problems with the trustee or judge regarding such a plan. Your retirement plan can be a vital asset and you should take all necessary steps to preserve it and protect it from your creditors.

WARNING: THE EXEMPTION CHARTS IN THIS APPENDIX ARE NOT GUARANTEED TO BE CURRENT, NOR ARE THEY GUARANTEED TO CONTAIN EVERY POSSIBLE EXEMPTION. THESE CHARTS ARE DESIGNED TO INCLUDE THE BASIC EXEMPTIONS TO COVER THE MOST USUAL SITUATIONS. LEGISLATURES MAY CHANGE THE EXEMPTIONS AT ANY TIME, AND THERE MAY BE OBSCURE EXEMPTIONS APPLICABLE TO VERY NARROW SITUATIONS. YOUR LOCAL PUBLIC LIBRARY, OR LAW LIBRARY (usually found at your county courthouse) SHOULD HAVE A CURRENT COPY OF YOUR STATE'S LAWS. YOUR LAW LIBRARY SHOULD ALSO HAVE BOOKS ABOUT BANKRUPTCY WHICH SHOULD CONTAIN THE MOST RECENT EXEMPTIONS. IF YOU THINK YOU HAVE A PARTICULAR ASSET WHICH MAY BE ENTITLED TO AN EXEMPTION NOT LISTED, OR FEEL YOU NEED AN EXEMPTION EXPLAINED IN MORE DETAIL, YOU SHOULD CONSULT AN ATTORNEY.

FEDERAL BANKRUPTCY EXEMPTIONS

The following Federal Bankruptcy Exemptions are available (as an alternative to the state exemptions) if you live in one of the following states:

Arkansas	Massachusetts	New Mexico	Texas
Connecticut	Michigan	Pennsylvania	Vermont
District of Columbia	Minnesota	Rhode Island	Washington
Hawaii	New Jersey	South Carolina	Wisconsin

If you use these exemptions, however, you cannot use the exemptions listed under your state. Be sure to compare these exemptions to those in the listing for your state, and use whichever allows you to keep more of your property. Remember, the Federal Bankruptcy Exemptions can be doubled by husband and wife.

The following section numbers relate to Title 11 of the United States Code, which is abbreviated "11 U.S.C." followed by the appropriate section ("§" is the symbol for "section" number.) An example is: "11 U.S.C. § 522(d)(1)." Only the section number is used below.

HOMESTEAD (**)
522(d)(1)   Real property, including mobile homes and coops, up to $15,000. Unused portion, up to $7,500, may be used for other property.

PERSONAL PROPERTY (**)
522(d)(2)   Motor vehicle up to $2,400.
522(d)(3)   Animals, crops, clothing, appliances and furnishings, books, household goods, and musical instruments up to $400 per item, and up to $8,000 total.
522(d)(4)   Jewelry up to $1,000.
522(d)(5) $800 of any property, and unused portion of homestead up to $7,500.
522(d)(9)   Health aids.
522(d)(11)(B) Wrongful death recovery for person you depended upon.
522(d)(11)(D) Personal injury recovery up to 15,000, except for pain and suffering or for pecuniary loss.
522(d)(11)(E) Lost earning payments.

PENSIONS
522(d)(10)(E) ERISA-qualified benefits needed for support.

PUBLIC BENEFITS
522(d)(10)(A) Public assistance, Social Security, Veteran's benefits, Unemployment Compensation.
522(d)(11)(A) Crime victim's compensation.

TOOLS OF TRADE (**)
522(d)(6)   Implements, books and tools of trade, up to $1,500.

ALIMONY AND CHILD SUPPORT
522(d)(10)(D) Alimony and child support needed for support.

INSURANCE
522(d)(7)   Unmatured life insurance policy.
522(d)(8)   Life insurance policy with loan value up to $8,000 (**).
522(d)(10)(C) Disability, unemployment or illness benefits.
522(d)(11)(C) Life insurance payments for a person you depended on, which you need for support.

FEDERAL NON-BANKRUPTCY EXEMPTIONS

You may only use these exemptions if you choose the exemptions listed under your state. You may not use these if you choose to use the Federal Bankruptcy Exemptions listed on the previous page.

RETIREMENT BENEFITS

50 U.S.C. §403	CIA employees.
5 U.S.C. §8346	Civil Service employees.
22 U.S.C. §4060	Foreign service employees.
10 U.S.C. §1440	Military service employees.
45 U.S.C.§.231m	Railroad workers.
42 U.S.C. §407	Social Security benefits.
38 U.S.C. §3101	Veteran's benefits.

SURVIVOR'S BENEFITS

10 U.S.C. §1450	Military service.
28 U.S.C. §376	Judges, U.S. court directors.
33 U.S.C. §775	Lighthouse workers.

DEATH AND DISABILITY BENEFITS

5 U.S.C. §8130	U.S. Government employees.
33 U.S.C. §916	Longshoremen, harbor workers.
42 U.S.C. §1717	Military service.

MISCELLANEOUS

10 U.S.C. §1035	Military deposits to savings accounts (while on permanent duty outside the U.S.).
15 U.S.C. §1673	75% of earned but unpaid wages (Judge may approve more).
25 U.S.C. §543 & 545	Klamath Indians tribe benefits.
38 U.S.C. §770(g)	Military group life insurance.
45 U.S.C. §352(e)	Railroad workers' unemployment.
46 U.S.C. §11110	Seamen's clothing.
46 U.S.C. §11111	Seamen's wages (while on a voyage and pursuant to a written contract).

ALABAMA

Code of Alabama, Title 6, Chapter 10 (C.A. §6-10-2). Ignore volume numbers; look for "title" numbers.

HOMESTEAD
6-10-2   Real property or mobile home, up to $5,000. Property can't exceed 160 acres.(**) Must record homestead declaration. 6-10-20.

PERSONAL PROPERTY
6-10-5   A burial place and a church pew or seat.

6-10-6   Clothing, books and family portraits and pictures, and $3,000 of any other personal property (except life insurance).

WAGES
6-10-7   75% of earned but unpaid wages. Judge may approve more for low-income debtors.

PENSIONS
12-18-10   Judges.   36-21-77   Law enforcement officers.
16-25-23   Teachers.   36-27-28   State employees.

PUBLIC BENEFITS
15-23-15   Crime victims' compensation.
25-4-140   Unemployment compensation.
25-5-86   Workers' compensation.
25-5-179   Coal miners' pneumoconiosis benefits.
31-7-2   Southeast Asian War POW's benefits.
38-4-8   AFDC and aid to blind, aged, and disabled.

TOOLS OF TRADE
31-2-78   Arms, uniforms and equipment required to be kept by state military personnel.

INSURANCE
6-10-8;
27-14-29   Life insurance proceeds if beneficiary is spouse or child of the insured.
27-14-31   Disability proceeds up to an average of $250 per month.
27-14-32   Annuities up to $250 per month.
27-15-26   Life insurance, if policy prohibits use to pay creditors.
27-30-25   Mutual aid association benefits.
27-34-27   Fraternal benefit society benefits.

MISCELLANEOUS
10-8-72   Business partnership property.
Other   Add any applicable Federal Non-Bankruptcy Exemptions.

ALASKA

Alaska Statutes, Title 9, Section 9.38.010 (A.S. §9.38.010). Ignore volume numbers; look for "title" numbers. In *In re McNutt*, 87 B.R. 84 (9th Cir. 1988), the Federal Bankruptcy Exemptions were allowed.

HOMESTEAD
9.38-010 (*) Up to $54,000.

PERSONAL PROPERTY
9.38.015   Burial plot; needed health aids; and tuition credits under advance college payment contract.
9.38.020   Motor vehicle up to $3,000, if market value is no more than $20,000; pets up to $1,000; jewelry up to $1,000; and household goods, clothing, books, musical instruments, and family portraits and heirlooms up to $3,000.
9.38.030   Personal injury and wrongful death recoveries, to the extent wages are exempt.
9.38.060   Proceeds from damaged exempt property.
34.35.105   Building materials.

WAGES
9.38.030;
9.38.050   Weekly net earnings up to $350, or up to $550 if sole wage earner in a household. If no regular pay, up to $1,400 paid in any month, or $2,200 if sole wage earner in household.

PENSIONS
9.38.015   Teachers, judicial & public employees, and elected officers, as to benefits accruing.
9.38.017   ERISA-qualified benefits, if deposited more than 120 days before filing.
9.38.030   Payments being received from other pensions.

PUBLIC BENEFITS
9.38.015   Alaska longevity bonus, crime victims' compensation and federally exempt public benefits.
23.20.405   Unemployment compensation.
23.30.160   Workers' compensation.
43.23.065   45% of Permanent Fund dividends (this is income distributed to residents from the state's natural resources).
47.25.210   General relief assistance.
47.25.395   AFDC.
47.25.550   Assistance to blind, elderly and disabled adults.

TOOLS OF TRADE
9.38.020   Implements, books or tools up to $2,800.

ALIMONY AND CHILD SUPPORT
9.38.015   Child support if received from a collection agency.
9.38.030   Alimony, to extent wages are exempt.

INSURANCE
9.38.015;
9.38.030   Medical and disability benefits.
9.38.025   Life insurance or annuity contracts up to a $10,000 loan value.
9.38.030   Life insurance proceeds to a spouse or dependent, and personal injury insurance proceeds, to extent wages are exempt.
21.84.240   Fraternal benefit society benefits.

MISCELLANEOUS
9.38.015   Liquor licenses; Alaska Fisheries limited entry permits.
9.38.100   Business partnership property.
Other   Add any applicable Federal Non-Bankruptcy Exemptions.

ARIZONA

Arizona Revised Statutes Annotated, Section 33-1101 (A.R.S. §33-1101). Ignore volume numbers; look for "section" numbers.

HOMESTEAD (*)
33-1101   Up to $100,000. Includes sale proceeds up to 18 months after sale, or new home purchased, whichever occurs first. Must record homestead declaration. 33-1102.

PERSONAL PROPERTY (**)
33-1123   The following items up to $4,000 total: Two beds; one bed table, dresser and lamp for each bed; bedding; kitchen table and 4 chairs; dining table and 4 chairs; living room chair for each family member; couch; 3 living room tables and lamps; living room carpet or rug; refrigerator; stove; washer and dryer; one TV, radio or stereo (not one of each); radio alarm clock; vacuum cleaner; family portraits; and any pictures, oil paintings, and drawings created by the debtor. Additional bed, and dining chair, for each additional dependent if more than 4 persons in household.

33-1124   Food and fuel for 6 months.

33-1125   Motor vehicle up to $1,500 (or $4,000 if disabled); clothing to $500; pets, horses, milk cows and poultry to $500; books to $250; wedding and engagement rings to $1,000; musical instruments to $250; watch to $100; wheelchair and prostheses; and up to $500 total for bicycle, sewing machine, typewriter, burial plot, firearm and bible (only one of each may be kept).

33-1126   Proceeds for sold or damaged exempt property; prepaid rent or security deposit to lesser of $1,000 or 1.5 times rent (only if not claiming homestead); bank deposit to $150 in one account.

WAGES
33-1126   Earnings of minor child, unless debt is for child.

33-1131   Minimum of 75% of unpaid net wages or pension payments. Judge may allow more.

PENSIONS
9-931   Police officers.

9-968   Firefighters.

15-1628   Members of board of regents.

33-1126   ERISA-qualified benefits, if deposited more than 120 days before filing [IRA's included, *In re Herrscher*, 121 B.R. 29 (D. Ariz. 1990)].

38-762   State employees.

38-811   Elected officials.

38-850   Public safety personnel.

41-955   Rangers.

PUBLIC BENEFITS
23-783   Unemployment compensation.

23-1068   Workers' compensation.

46-208   Welfare benefits.

TOOLS OF TRADE
33-1127   Teaching aids of a teacher.

33-1130 (**)   Tools, equipment and books up to $2,500; Farm machinery, utensils, instruments of husbandry, feed, seed, grain and animals up to a total value of $2,500; and arms, uniforms and equipment you are required by law to keep.

INSURANCE
20-881   Fraternal benefit society benefits.

20-1131   Life insurance cash value up to $2,000 per dependent/$10,000 total.

20-1132   Group life insurance policy or proceeds.

33-1126 (**)   Life insurance proceeds if beneficiary is spouse or child, up to $20,000; life insurance cash value to $1,000 per dependent/$25,000 total; and health, accident or disability benefits.

MISCELLANEOUS
29-225   Business partnership property.

Other   Add any applicable Federal Non-Bankruptcy Exemptions.

ARKANSAS

Arkansas Code of 1987 Annotated, Title 16, Chapter 66, Section 16-66-210 (A.C.A. §16-66-210). Ignore volume numbers; look for "title" and "chapter" numbers. Compare Federal Bankruptcy Exemptions.

HOMESTEAD (Choose one of the following)

16-66-210 (*)   Head of family may claim: Real or personal property used as a residence; of up to 1/4 acre in a city, town, or village; or up to 80 acres elsewhere. If between 1/4 and 1 acre in city, etc., or 80 to 160 acres elsewhere, amount of exemption in limited to $2,500. No homestead may exceed 1 acre in city, etc., or 160 acres elsewhere. This exemption is also found in the State Constitution, and the reference to "Ark. Const. 9-3, 9-4, & 9-5" should also be used.

16-66-218   Real or personal property used as a residence, up to $800 if single or $1,250 if married. Also, $500 of any personal property, if married or head of household; $200 if single (cite "Ark. Const. 9-1; 9-2" also).

PERSONAL PROPERTY (also see §16-66-218 under the homestead section above)

16-66-218   Motor vehicle up to $1,200, and wedding bands provided that any diamonds can't exceed 1/2 carat.

16-66-207   Burial plot up to 5 acres, provided you don't use homestead exemption in section 16-66-218.

Ark. Const.   Clothing of unlimited value; and any personal property of up to $500 if married or head of family, or $200 otherwise. Use reference to "Ark. Const. 9-1 & 9-2."

WAGES

16-66-208   Earned but unpaid wages due for 60 days, but in not less than $25 per week.

PENSIONS

16-66-218   IRA deposits up to $20,000 if deposited over 1 year before filing for bankruptcy.
24-6-223   State police officers.
24-7-715   School employees.
24-10-616   Police officers and firefighters.
24-11-417   Disabled police officers.
24-11-814   Disabled firefighters.

PUBLIC BENEFITS

11-9-110   Worker's compensation.
11-10-109   Unemployment compensation.
16-90-716   Crime victims' compensation, unless you are seeking to discharge a debt for treatment of an injury incurred during the crime.
20-76-430   AFDC, and aid to blind, aged or disabled.

TOOLS OF TRADE

16-66-218   Tools, books and implements of trade to $750.

INSURANCE

16-66-209   Life, health, accident or disability proceeds, whether paid or due (case law limits to $500).
23-71-112   Stipulated insurance premiums.
23-72-114   Mutual assessment life or disability benefits up to $1,000.
23-74-119   Fraternal benefit society benefits.
23-79-131   Life insurance proceeds if beneficiary isn't the insured; life insurance proceeds if policy prohibits proceeds from being used to pay beneficiary's creditors.
23-79-132   Group life insurance.
23-79-133   Disability benefits.
23-79-134   Annuity contract.

MISCELLANEOUS

4-42-502   Business partnership property.
Other   Add any applicable Federal Non-Bankruptcy Exemptions.

CALIFORNIA

West's Annotated California Codes, Civil Procedure, Section 704.710 (Cal. Code Civ. Proc. §704.710). California has two separate systems of exemptions. You must select one, and cannot mix exemptions from the two systems. References are to the California Code of Civil Procedure unless otherwise stated (look for volume marked "Civil Procedure," not just "Civil").

CALIFORNIA (SYSTEM 1)

HOMESTEAD

Real or personal property occupied at time of filing for bankruptcy, including mobile home, boat, stock cooperative, community apartment, planned development or condominium, up to the following limits: $50,000 if single and not disabled; $75,000 if family and no other member has homestead; $100,000 if 65 or older or if physically or mentally disabled; $100,000 if creditors are seeking to force sale of your home and you are either (a)55 or older, single and earn under $15,000 per year, or (b)55 or older, married and earn under $20,000 per year. Sale proceeds are exempt for up to 6 months after sale. (*)

PERSONAL PROPERTY

704.010	Motor vehicle or insurance if vehicle lost, destroyed or damaged up to $1,900 (*).
704.020	Food, clothing, appliances and furnishings.
704.030	Building materials to repair or improve home up to $2,000 (*).
704.040	Jewelry, heirlooms and art up to $5,000 total (*).
704.050	Health aids.
704.080	Bank deposits from Social Security Administration up to $2,000 for single payee ($3,000 for husband and wife payees); proceeds from exempt property in form of cash or bank deposits.
704.090	Inmates trust funds up to $1,000.
704.140	Personal injury causes of action, and recoveries needed for support.
704.150	Wrongful death causes of action, and recoveries needed for support.
704.200	Burial plot

WAGES

704.070	75% of wages paid within 30 days prior to filing bankruptcy.
704.113	Public employee vacation credits (75% minimum if receiving installment payments).

PENSIONS

704.110	Public retirement benefits.
704.115	Private retirements benefits to extent tax-deferred, including IRA and Keogh.
Gov't. 21201	Public employees.
Gov't. 31452	County employees.
Gov't. 31913	County peace officers.
Gov't. 32210	County fire fighters.

PUBLIC BENEFITS

704.120	Unemployment benefits and union benefits due to labor dispute.
704.160	Workers' compensation.
704.170	AFDC and aid to blind, aged and disabled.
704.180	Relocation benefits.
704.190	Financial aid to students.

TOOLS OF TRADE

704.060	Tools, implements, materials, books, uniforms, instruments, equipment, furnishings, motor vehicle, and vessel up to $5,000, or up to $10,000 if used by both spouses in the same occupation. Can't claim motor vehicle here if already claimed under 704.010.

[CONTINUED ON NEXT PAGE]

INSURANCE

704.100 (**) Matured life insurance benefits needed for support of unlimited value, unmatured life insurance policy up to $4,000 in value, and fraternal life insurance benefits to $4,000.

704.120   Fraternal unemployment benefits.

704.130   Disability or health benefits.

704.720   Homeowners' insurance proceeds for 6 months after received, up to amount of homestead.

Other   Fidelity bonds. Refer to as "Labor 404."

Other   Life insurance proceeds if policy prohibits use to pay creditors. Refer to as "Ins. 10132, 10170 & 10171."

MISCELLANEOUS

Corp. 15025 Business partnership property.

Other   Add any applicable Federal Non-Bankruptcy Exemptions.

CALIFORNIA (SYSTEM 2) [no doubling of any exemptions]

HOMESTEAD

703.140(b)(1)   Real or personal property (e.g., mobile home), including co-op, used as a residence up to $15,000.

PERSONAL PROPERTY

703.140(b)(1)   Burial plot up to $15,000, instead of homestead.

703.140(b)(2)   Motor vehicle up to $2,400.

703.140(b)(3)   Clothing, household goods, appliances, furnishings, animals, books, musical instruments and crops up to $400 per item.

703.140(b)(4)   Jewelry up to $1,000.

703.140(b)(5) $15,000 of any property, less any claim for homestead or burial plot.

703.140(b)(5) $800 of any property.

703.140(b)(9)   Health aids.

703.140(b)(11)   Wrongful death recoveries needed for support.

703.140(b)(11)   Personal injury recoveries up to $15,000, not to include pain, suffering or pecuniary loss.

PENSIONS

703.140(b)(10)   ERISA-qualified benefits needed for support.

PUBLIC BENEFITS

703.140(b)(10)   Unemployment compensation, social security, and public assistance.

703.140(b)(10)   Veterans' benefits.

703.140(b)(11)   Crime victims' compensation.

TOOLS OF TRADE

703.140(b)(6)   Tools, books and implements of trade up to $1,500.

ALIMONY AND CHILD SUPPORT

703.140(b)(10)   Alimony and child support needed for support.

INSURANCE

703.140(b)(7)   Unmatured life insurance policy, other than credit.

703.140(b)(8)   Unmatured life insurance contract accrued interest, dividends, loan, cash or surrender value up to $8,000.

703.140(b)(10)   Disability benefits.

703.140(b)(11)   Life insurance proceeds needed for support.

Other   Fidelity bonds. Refer to as "Labor 404."

MISCELLANEOUS

695.060   Business and professional licenses, except liquor licenses.

Other   Add any applicable Federal Non-Bankruptcy Exemptions.

COLORADO

West's Colorado Revised Statutes Annotated, Title 13, Article 54, Section 13-54-102 (C.R.S.A. §13-54-102).

HOMESTEAD
13-54-102 Mobile home used as residence up to $6,000 value; house trailer or coach used as residence up to $3,500.

38-41-201 Real property, including mobile or manufactured home if loan incurred after 1/1/83, up to $30,000. For homestead exemption, must be occupied at time petition is filed. Sale proceeds are exempt for 1 year after sale. Spouse or child of deceased owner can also qualify.

PERSONAL PROPERTY
13-54-102 Motor vehicles to $1,000 to get to work (up to $3,000 to get medical care if elderly or disabled); clothing to $750; health aids; household goods to $1,500; food and fuel to $300; 1 burial plot per person; jewelry and articles of adornment to $500 total; pictures and books to $750; security deposit; proceeds for damaged exempt property; personal injury recoveries, unless debt related to the injury.

WAGES
13-54-104 Minimum 75% of earned but unpaid wages, and pension payments. Judge may approve more for low income debtors.

PENSIONS
13-54-102	ERISA-qualified benefits, including IRA's.
22-64-120	Teachers.
24-51-212	Public employees.
31-30-313;31-30-616	Police officers.
31-30-412;31-30-518	Firefighters.

PUBLIC BENEFITS
8-80-103	Unemployment compensation.
8-52-107	Workers' compensation.
13-54-102	Veterans' benefits for veteran, spouse or child if veteran served in war.
13-54-102;24-4.1-114	Crime victims' compensation.
26-2-131	AFDC, aid to blind, aged and disabled.

TOOLS OF TRADE
13-54-102 Stock in trade, supplies, fixtures, machines, tools, maps, equipment and books to $1,500 total; library of a professional to $1,500; livestock and poultry of a farmer to $3,000; horses, mules, wagons, carts, machinery, harness and tools of farmer to $2,000 total.

ALIMONY AND CHILD SUPPORT
13-54-102.5 Child support if recipient doesn't mix with other funds, or if deposited in a separate account for the child's benefit.

INSURANCE
10-7-106	Life insurance proceeds if policy prohibits use to pay creditors.
10-7-205	Group life insurance policy or proceeds.
10-8-114	Disability benefits up to $200 per month.
10-14-122	Fraternal benefit society benefits.
13-54-102	Life insurance dividends, interest, cash or surrender value up to $5,000.
38-41-209	Homeowners' insurance proceeds for 1 year after received, up to homestead amount.

MISCELLANEOUS
7-60-125	Business partnership property.
Other	Add any applicable Federal Non-Bankruptcy Exemptions.

CONNECTICUT

Connecticut General Statutes Annotated, Title 52, Section 52-352B (C.G.S.A. §52-352B). Ignore volume and "chapter" numbers; look for "title" and section numbers. Compare federal exemptions.

HOMESTEAD
52-352b   Real property, including mobile or manufactured home, up to $75,000.

PERSONAL PROPERTY
52-352b   Motor vehicle up to $1,500; food, clothing and health aids; appliances, furniture and bedding; wedding and engagement rings; burial plot; residential utility and security deposits for 1 residence; proceeds for damaged exempt property; and $1,000 of any property.

WAGES
52-361a   Minimum 75% of earned but unpaid wages. Judge may approve more for low income debtors.

PENSIONS
5-171;5-192w   State employees.
10-183q   Teachers.
52-352b   ERISA-qualified benefits, but only as to payments received and only to the extent wages are exempt.

PUBLIC BENEFITS
7-446   Municipal employees.
27-140   Vietnam veterans' death benefits.
31-272; 52-352b   Unemployment compensation.
45-48   Probate judges and employees.
52-352b   Workers' compensation; veterans' benefits; social security; wages from earnings incentive programs; AFDC; aid to blind, aged and disabled.
52-352b; 54-213   Crime victims' compensation.

TOOLS OF TRADE
52-352b   Arms, military equipment, uniforms and musical instruments of military personnel; tools, books, instruments and farm animals needed. Farm animals and livestock feed reasonably required, and moneys due from insurance on such property, owned by a farm partnership where at least 50% of the partners are members of the same family.

ALIMONY AND CHILD SUPPORT
52-352b   Alimony and child support, to extent wages are exempt.

INSURANCE
38a-380   Benefits under no-fault insurance law, to extent wages are exempt.
38a-453   Life insurance proceeds, dividends, interest, or cash or surrender value.
38a-454   Life insurance proceeds if policy prohibits use to pay creditors.
38a-636   Fraternal benefit society benefits.
52-352b   Health and disability benefits; disability benefits paid by association for its members; unmatured life insurance policy dividends, interest, or loan value up to $4,000, if you or a person on whom you are dependent is the person whose life is insured.

MISCELLANEOUS
34-63   Business partnership property.

DELAWARE

Delaware Code Annotated, Title 10, Section 4902 (D.C.A. 10 §4902). Ignore volume numbers; look for "title" numbers.

LIMITATION:

10 §4914   Total exemptions for a single person may not exceed $5,000; and for husband and wife may not exceed $10,000.

HOMESTEAD

Tenancies by the entirety exempt without limitation as to debts of one spouse. [In re *Hovatter*, 25 B.R. 123 (D. Del. 1982)].

PERSONAL PROPERTY

10 §4902; 10 §4903

Clothing, including jewelry; books; family pictures; piano; leased organs and sewing machines; burial plot; church pew or any seat in public place of worship. Also $500 of any other personal property if head of family (except tools of trade). School books & family library.

WAGES

10 §4913   85% of earned but unpaid wages.

PENSIONS

9 §4316   Kent County employees.
11 §8803   Police officers.
16 §6653   Volunteer firefighters.
29 §5503   State employees.

PUBLIC BENEFITS

19 §2355   Workers' compensation.
19 §3374   Unemployment compensation.
31 §513   General assistance; AFDC; aid to aged and disabled.
31 §2309   Aid to blind.

TOOLS OF TRADE

10 §4902   Tools, implements and fixtures, up to $75 in New Castle and Sussex counties, and up to $50 in Kent County.

INSURANCE

12 §1901   Employee life insurance benefits.
18 §2726   Health or disability benefits.
18 §2727   Group life insurance policy or proceeds.
18 §2728   Annuity contract proceeds up to $350 per month.
18 §2729   Life insurance proceeds if policy prohibits use to pay creditors.
18 §6118   Fraternal benefit society benefits.

MISCELLANEOUS

6 §1525   Business partnership property.
Other   Add any applicable Federal Non-Bankruptcy Exemptions.

DISTRICT OF COLUMBIA

D.C. Code, Title 45, Section 1869 (D.C.C. §45-1869). Ignore "Chapter" number; look for "title" number. Compare federal exemptions.

HOMESTEAD
45-1869   Residential condominium deposit. Tenancies by the entirety exempt without limit as to debts of one spouse [*Estate of Wall*, 440 F.2d 215 (D.C.Cir. 1971)].

PERSONAL PROPERTY
15-501   Clothing up to $300 (also refer to 15-503); beds, bedding, radios, cooking utensils, stoves, furniture, furnishings and sewing machines up to $300 total; books to $400; family pictures; food and fuel to last 3 months.

29-1128   Cooperative association holding to $50.

WAGES
15-503   Non-wage, earnings, including pensions, for 60 days up to $200 per month for head of family, or $60 per month otherwise.

16-572   Minimum 75% of earned but unpaid wages or pension payments.

PENSIONS
11-1570   Judges.

31-1217; 31-1238   Public school teachers.

PUBLIC BENEFITS
3-215.1   General assistance; AFDC; aid to blind, aged and disabled.

3-407   Crime victims' compensation.

36-317   Workers' compensation.

46-119   Unemployment compensation.

TOOLS OF TRADE
1-806   Seal and documents of notary public.

15-501   Motor vehicle, cart, wagon or dray, horse or mule harness up to $500; stock and materials to $200; library, furniture, tools of professional or artist to $300.

15-501;15-503   Mechanic's tools, tools of trade or business to $200.

INSURANCE
15-503   Other insurance proceeds to $200 per month, for a maximum of 2 months, for head of family; up to $60 per month otherwise.

35-521   Life insurance proceeds, dividends, interest, cash or surrender value.

35-522   Disability benefits.

35-523   Group life insurance policy or proceeds.

35-525   Life insurance proceeds if policy prohibits use to pay creditors.

35-1211   Fraternal benefit society benefits.

MISCELLANEOUS
41-124   Business partnership property.

Other   Add any applicable Federal Non-Bankruptcy Exemptions.

FLORIDA

Florida Statutes, Chapter 222, Section 222.05 (F.S. §222.05). Ignore volume numbers; look for "chapter" numbers.

HOMESTEAD

222.05 Real or personal property, including mobile or modular home and condominium, to unlimited value. Property cannot exceed 1/2 acre in a municipality, or 160 acres elsewhere. Spouse or child of deceased owner may claim exemption. (Also refer to Florida Constitution, as "Fla. Const. 10-4."). Also, tenancies by the entireties in real property are exempt as to debts of one spouse [In re *Avins*, 19 B.R. 736 (S.D.Fla. 1982)].

PERSONAL PROPERTY

222.25 Motor vehicle up to $1,000; prescribed health aids.

Other Any personal property up to $1,000 total. (Refer to as "Fla. Const. 10-4")(**).

WAGES

222.11 Earned but unpaid wages, or wages paid and in a bank account, only if head of household.

222.21 Federal government employees pension payments needed for support and received 3 months before filing bankruptcy.

PENSIONS

112.215 Government employees' deferred compensation plans.

121.131 State officers and employees.

122.15 County officers and employees.

175.241 Firefighters.

185.25 Police officers.

222.21 Retirement plans under various sections of Internal Revenue Code. Includes pension, profit sharing and stock bonus plans under §401(a); annuity plans [§403(a)]; educational annuities [§403(b)]; IRAs [§408]; and employee stock ownership plans [§409]. Also, ERISA-qualified benefits.

238.15 Teachers.

321.22 Highway patrol officers.

PUBLIC BENEFITS

222.201 Public assistance and social security.

222.201; 443.051 Unemployment compensation.

222.201; 744.626 Veterans' benefits.

440.22 Workers' compensation.

769.05 Proceeds for job-related injuries under Chapter 769 relating to hazardous occupations.

960.14 Crime victims' compensation unless seeking to discharge debt for treatment of crime related injury.

ALIMONY AND CHILD SUPPORT

222.201 Alimony and child support needed for support.

INSURANCE

222.13 Death benefits payable to a specific beneficiary.

222.14 Annuity contract proceeds and life insurance cash surrender value.

222.18 Disability or illness benefits.

632.619 Fraternal benefit society benefits, if received before 10/1/96.

MISCELLANEOUS

222.22 Funds paid to the Prepaid Postsecondary Education Trust Fund program.

497.413 Funds the debtor may be entitled to from the Florida Department of Banking and Finance Preneed Funeral Contract Consumer Protection Trust Fund.

620.68 Business partnership property.

Other Add any applicable Federal Non-Bankruptcy Exemptions.

GEORGIA

Official Code of Georgia Annotated, Title 44, Chapter 13, Section 1 (C.G.A. §44-13-100). [This is not the same set as the "Georgia Code," which is a separate set of books with a completely different numbering system.] Ignore volume numbers; look for "title" and "chapter" numbers.

HOMESTEAD
44-13-100   Real or personal property, including coop, used as a residence up to $5,000. Unused portion may be applied to any other property.

PERSONAL PROPERTY
44-13-100   Motor vehicles up to $1,000; clothing, household goods, appliances, furnishings, books, musical instruments, animals and crops up to $200 per item, and $3,500 total; jewelry up to $500; health aids; lost future earnings needed for support; personal injury recoveries up to $7,500; wrongful death recoveries needed for support. Also, burial plot in lieu of homestead. Also, $400 of any property.

WAGES
18-4-20   Minimum 75% of earned but unpaid wages for private and federal government workers. Judge may approve more for low income debtors.

PENSIONS
18-4-22   ERISA-qualified benefits.
47-2-332   Public employees.
44-13-100   Other pensions needed for support, but only as to payments being received.

PUBLIC BENEFITS
44-13-100   Unemployment compensation, veterans' benefits, social security, crime victims' compensation, and local public assistance.
49-4-35   Old age assistance.
49-4-58   Aid to blind.
49-4-84   Workers' compensation; aid to disabled.

TOOLS OF TRADE
44-13-100   Tools, books and implements of trade up to $500.

ALIMONY AND CHILD SUPPORT
44-13-100   Alimony and child support needed for support.

INSURANCE
44-13-100   Unmatured life insurance contract, unmatured life insurance dividends, interest, loan value or cash value up to $2,000 if you or someone you depend on is beneficiary, life insurance proceeds if policy is owned by someone you depend on and is needed for support.
33-15-20   Fraternal benefit society benefits.
33-25-11   Life insurance proceeds, dividends, interest, loan, cash or surrender value, provided that beneficiary is not the insured.
33-28-7   Annuity and endowment contract benefits.
33-27-7   Group insurance.
33-26-5   Industrial life insurance policy owned by someone you depend on for support.
33-29-15   Disability or health benefits up to $250 per month.

MISCELLANEOUS
Other   Add any applicable Federal Non-Bankruptcy Exemptions.

HAWAII

Hawaii Revised Statutes Annotated, Chapter 36, Title 651, Section 36-651-92 (H.R.S. §36-651-92). Ignore volume numbers; look for "chapter" and "title" numbers. Compare federal exemptions.

HOMESTEAD
36-651-91;

36-651-92   Up to $30,000 if head of family or over 65; up to $20,000 otherwise. Property can't exceed 1 acre (includes long-term leased land). Sale proceeds are exempt for 6 months after sale. Tenancies by the entirety are exempt without limit as to debts of one spouse [*Security Pacific Bank v. Chang*, 818 F.Supp. (D. Haw. 1993)].

PERSONAL PROPERTY
20-359-104   Down payment for home in state project.

36-651-121   Motor vehicle up to wholesale value of $1,000; clothing; appliances and furnishings needed; books; jewelry and articles of adornment up to $1,000; proceeds for sold or damaged exempt property (sale proceeds exempt for 6 months after sale); burial plot up to 250 square feet, plus on-site tombstones, monuments and fencing

WAGES
20-353-22   Prisoner's wages held by Dept. of Public Safety.

36-651-121;

36-652-1   Unpaid wages due for services of the past 31 days. If more than 31 days, 95% of first $100, 90% of second $100, and 80% of balance.

PENSIONS
7-88-91;

36-653-3   Public officers and employees.

36-651-124   ERISA-qualified benefits, if deposited more than 3 years before filing.

7-88-169   Police officers and firefighters.

PUBLIC BENEFITS
20-346-33   Public assistance paid by Dept. of Public Safety.

21-383-163   Unemployment compensation.

21-386-57   Workers' compensation.

36-653-4   Unemployment work relief up to $60 per month.

TOOLS OF TRADE
36-651-121   Tools, books, uniforms, implements, instruments, furnishings, fishing boat, nets, motor vehicle and other personal property needed for livelihood.

INSURANCE
24-431:10-231   Disability benefits.

24-431:10-232   Annuity contract or endowment policy proceeds if beneficiary is insured spouse, child or parent.

24-431:10-233   Group life insurance policy or proceeds.

24-431:10-234   Life or health insurance policy for child.

24-431:10-D:112   Life insurance proceeds if policy prohibits use to pay creditors.

24-432:2-403   Fraternal benefit society benefits.

MISCELLANEOUS
23-425-125   Business partnership property.

IDAHO

Idaho Code, Title 55, Section 55-1201 (I.C. §55-1201). Ignore volume number.

HOMESTEAD (*)
55-1003 $50,000. Sale and insurance proceeds are exempt for 1 year (55-1008). Before filing for bankruptcy, you must file a homestead declaration (55-1004).

PERSONAL PROPERTY
11-603   Health aids; burial plot.

11-604   Personal injury and wrongful death recoveries needed for support.

11-605   Motor vehicle up to $1,500; jewelry up to $250; clothing, pets, appliances, furnishings, books, musical instruments, 1 firearm, family portraits and sentimental heirlooms up to $500 per item, but only up to $4,000 total; crops cultivated by the debtor on up to 50 acres (including water rights up to 160 inches) to $1,000.

11-606   Proceeds for damaged exempt property, for up to 3 months after received.

45-514   Building materials.

WAGES
11-207   Minimum of 75% of earned but unpaid wages and pension payments. Judge may approve more for low income debtors.

PENSIONS
11-604   Payments being received from pensions needed for support, provided payments are not mixed with other money.

50-1517   Police officers.

55-1011   ERISA-qualified benefits.

59-1325   Public employees.

72-1417   Firefighters.

PUBLIC BENEFITS
11-603   Unemployment compensation, social security, veterans' benefits, and federal, state and local public assistance.

56-223   General assistance, AFDC, and aid to blind, aged and disabled.

72-802   Workers' compensation.

72-1020   Crime victims' compensation, unless debt related to injury sustained during the crime, and only as to benefits received before 6/30/91, as law has since been repealed.

TOOLS OF TRADE
11-605   Tools, books and implements of trade up to $1,000; arms, uniforms and accoutrements required to be kept by peace officer, national guard or military personnel.

ALIMONY AND CHILD SUPPORT
11-604   Alimony and child support needed for support.

INSURANCE
11-603   Medical or hospital care benefits

11-604;41-1833;

41-1834   Death and disability benefits; life insurance if insured in not the beneficiary.

41-1830   Life insurance policy if the beneficiary is a married woman.

41-1833   Life insurance proceeds, dividends, interest, loan, cash or surrender value if the insured is not the beneficiary.

41-1835   Group life insurance benefits.

41-1836   Annuity contract proceeds up to $350 per month.

41-1930   Life insurance proceeds if policy prohibits use to pay creditors.

41-3218   Fraternal benefit society benefits.

MISCELLANEOUS
53-325   Business partnership property.

ILLINOIS

West's Smith-Hurd Illinois Compiled Statutes Annotated, Chapter 735, Act 5, Article 12, Section 5/12-901 (735-5/12-901). Paragraph 12-901 (I.A.S. 110 ¶12-901). Look for "chapter" numbers.

HOMESTEAD (**)
735-5/12-901 Real or personal property, including a farm, lot and buildings, condominium, coop or mobile home, up to $7,500. Spouse or child of deceased owner can claim homestead (735-5/12-902). Sale proceeds up to 1 year (735-5/12-906).

PERSONAL PROPERTY
625-45/3A-7(d) Title certificate for a boat more than 12 feet in length.
735-5/12-1001 Motor vehicle up to $1,200; clothing needed; prescribed health aids; school books; family pictures; bible; personal injury recoveries up to $7,500; wrongful death recoveries needed for support; proceeds from sale of exempt property; any other personal property up to $2,000 (including wages).

WAGES
740-170/4 Minimum 85% of earned but unpaid wages. Judge may approve more for low income debtor.

PENSIONS

40-5/2-154	General assembly members.	50-5/15-185	State university
40-5/3-144; 40-5/5-218	Police officers.	40-5/18-161	Judges.
40-5/4-135; 40-5/6-213	Firefighters.	40-5/19-117	House of correction
40-5/7-217; 40-5/8-244	Municipal employees.		employees.
40-5/9-228	County employees.	40-5/19-218	Public library employees.
40-5/11-223	Civil service employees.	40-5/22-230	Disabled firefighters, and
40-5/12-190	Park employees.		widows and children of
40-5/13-808	Sanitation district employees.		firefighters.
40-5/14-147	State employees.	735-5/12-1006	ERISA-qualified benefits;
50-5/15-185	State university employees.		and public employees.
50-5/16-190; 40-5/17-151	Teachers.		

PUBLIC BENEFITS
305-5/11-3 AFDC; aid to blind, aged and disabled.
820-305-21 Workers' compensation.
820-310/21 Workers' occupational disease compensation.
735-5/12-1001 Veterans' benefits; social security; unemployment compensation; crime victims' compensation; restitution payments for World War II relocation of Japanese Americans and Aleuts under the federal Civil Liberties Act of 1988 and the Aleution and Pribilof Island Restitution Act.

TOOLS OF TRADE
735-5/12-1001 Tools, books and implements of trade up to $750.

ALIMONY AND CHILD SUPPORT
735-5/12-1001 Alimony and child support needed for support.

INSURANCE
215-5/238 Life insurance, annuity or cash value if beneficiary is spouse, child, parent, or other dependent; life insurance proceeds if policy prohibits use to pay creditors.
215-5/299.1a Fraternal benefit society benefits.
735-5/12-907 Homeowners' insurance proceeds for destroyed home, up to $7,500.
735-5/12-1001 Health and disability benefits, life insurance proceeds needed for support, and life insurance policy if beneficiary is spouse or child.

MISCELLANEOUS
805-205/25 Business partnership property.
Other Add any applicable Federal Non-Bankruptcy Exemptions.

INDIANA

West's Annotated Indiana Code, Title 34, Article 2, Chapter 28, Section 1 (A.I.C. §34-2-28-1). Look for "title" numbers.

HOMESTEAD
34-2-28-1   Real or personal property used as a residence up to $7,500 (LIMIT: Homestead plus personal property can't exceed $10,000, not including health aids); tenancies by the entirety exempt without limit unless bankruptcy is seeking to discharge debts incurred by both spouses.

PERSONAL PROPERTY
34-2-28-1   Health aids; up to $4,000 of real or tangible personal property; up to $100 of intangible personal property (except for money owed to you).

WAGES
24-4.5-5-105 Minimum of 75% of earned but unpaid wages. Judge may approve more for low income debtors.

PENSIONS
5-10.3-8-9	Public employees.
10-1-2-9; 36-8-8-17	Police officers, but only as to benefits accruing.
21-6.1-5-17	State teachers.
34-2-28-1	Public or private retirement benefits.
36-8-7-22; 36-8-8-17	Firefighters.
36-8-10-19	Sheriffs, but only benefits accruing.

PUBLIC BENEFITS
16-7-3.6-15   Crime victims' compensation, unless seeking to discharge debt for treatment of crime-related injury.
22-3-2-17   Workers' compensation.
22-4-33-3   Unemployment compensation.

TOOLS OF TRADE
10-2-6-3   National guard arms, uniforms and equipment.

INSURANCE
27-1-12-14   Life insurance policy or proceeds if beneficiary is spouse or dependent.
27-1-12-29   Group life insurance policy.
27-2-5-1   Life insurance proceeds if policy prohibits use to pay creditors.
27-8-3-23   Mutual life or accident policy proceeds.
27-11-6-3   Fraternal benefit society benefits.

MISCELLANEOUS
23-4-1-25   Business partnership property.
Other   Add any applicable Federal Non-Bankruptcy Exemptions.

IOWA

Iowa Code Annotated, Section 499A.18 (I.C.A. §449A.18). Ignore volume numbers; look for "section" numbers.

HOMESTEAD
499A.18; 561.2; 561.16   Real property or apartment, unlimited in value, but cannot exceed 1/2 acre in a city or town, or 40 acres elsewhere.

PERSONAL PROPERTY
627.6   Motor vehicle, musical instruments and tax refunds up to $5,000 total (but tax refund portion limited to $1,000 of the total); clothing up to $1,000, plus receptacles to hold clothing; household goods, appliances, and furnishings up to $2,000 total; wedding and engagement rings; books, portraits, paintings and pictures up to $1,000; health aids; burial plot up to 1 acre; rifle or musket; shotgun; up to $100 of any other personal property including cash.

WAGES
642.21   Minimum of 75% of earned but unpaid wages and pension payments. Judge may approve more for low income debtors.

PENSIONS
97A-12   Peace officers.
97B-39   Public employees.
410.11   Disabled firefighters and police officers, but only for benefits being received.
411.13   Police officers and firefighters.
627.6   Pensions needed for support, but only as to payments being received, including IRAs.
627.8   Federal government pension, but only as to payments being received.

PUBLIC BENEFITS
627.6   Unemployment compensation, veterans' benefits, social security, AFDC, and local public assistance.
627.13   Workers' compensation.
627.19   Adopted child assistance.

TOOLS OF TRADE
627.6   Non-farming equipment up to $10,000; farming equipment, including livestock and feed, up to $10,000; but not including a car.

ALIMONY AND CHILD SUPPORT
627.6   Alimony and child support needed for support.

INSURANCE
508.32   Life insurance proceeds if policy prohibits use to pay creditors.
509.12   Employee group insurance policy or proceeds.
627.6   Life insurance proceeds up to $10,000, (if acquired within 2 years prior to filing for bankruptcy); and accident, disability, health, illness or life proceeds, dividends, interest, loan, cash or surrender value up to $15,000; if beneficiary is spouse, child or other dependent.

MISCELLANEOUS
123.38   Liquor licenses.
544.25   Business partnership property.
Other   Add any applicable Federal Non-Bankruptcy Exemptions.

KANSAS

Kansas Statutes Annotated, Section 60-2301 (K.S.A. §60-2301). Ignore volume numbers; look for "section" numbers. You may find either "*Vernon's* Kansas Statutes Annotated," or "Kansas Statutes Annotated, Official." The most recent law will be in the supplements, which is a pocket part in "*Vernon's*" and a separate soft-cover volume in the "Official." Both have a poor index.

HOMESTEAD
60-2301   Real property or mobile home of unlimited value, but can't exceed 1 acre in a city or town, or 160 acres on a farm. You must occupy or intend to occupy the property at the time you file for bankruptcy. (Also refer to "Const. 15-9").

PERSONAL PROPERTY
60-2304   Motor vehicle up to $20,000 (no limit if equipped or designed for a disabled person); clothing to last 1 year; household equipment and furnishings; food and fuel to last 1 year; jewelry and articles of adornment up to $1,000; burial plot.
16-310   Funeral plan prepayments.

WAGES
60-2310   Minimum of 75% of earned but unpaid wages. Judge may approve more for low income debtor.

PENSIONS
12-5005; 13-14a10   Police officers.
12-5005; 14-10a10   Firefighters.
13-14,102   Elected and appointed officials in cities with populations of between 120,000 and 200,000.
60-2308   Federal government pension needed for support and received within 3 months prior to filing bankruptcy; ERISA-qualified benefits.
72-5526   State school employees.
74-2618   Judges.
74-4923; 74-49,105   Public employees.
74-4989   State highway patrol officers.

PUBLIC BENEFITS
39-717   AFDC; general assistance; social welfare.
44-514   Workers' compensation.
44-718   Unemployment compensation.
74-7313   Crime victims' compensation.

TOOLS OF TRADE
48-245   National guard uniforms, arms and equipment.
60-2304   Equipment, instruments, furniture, books, documents, breeding stock, seed, stock and grain up to $7,500 total.

INSURANCE
40-258   Life insurance proceeds up to $1,000, but only if payable to the decedent's estate.
40-414   Life insurance proceeds or cash value deposited into a bank account; life insurance forfeiture value, only if policy issued over 1 year prior to filing for bankruptcy; fraternal benefit society benefits.
40-414a   Life insurance proceeds if policy prohibits use to pay creditors.

MISCELLANEOUS
41-326   Liquor licenses.
56-325   Business partnership property.
Other   Add any applicable Federal Non-Bankruptcy Exemptions.

KENTUCKY

Kentucky Revised Statutes. Chapter 427, Section 060 (K.R.S. §427.060). Ignore volume numbers; look for "chapter" numbers.

HOMESTEAD
427.060   Real or personal property used as a family residence up to $5,000. Sale proceeds are also exempt (427.060).

PERSONAL PROPERTY
304.39-260   Reparation benefits received and medical expenses paid under motor vehicle reparation law.
427.010   Motor vehicle up to $2,500; health aids; clothing, furniture, jewelry and articles of adornment up to $3,000 total.
427.060   Burial plot up to $5,000, in lieu of homestead.
427.150   Lost earnings payments needed for support; wrongful death recoveries for person you depended upon for support; personal injury recoveries up to $7,500, but not including pain, suffering or pecuniary loss.
427.160 $1,000 of any property.

WAGES
427.101   Minimum of 75% of earned but unpaid wages. Judge may approve more for low income debtor.

PENSIONS
61.690   State employees.
67A.350   Urban county government employees.
67A.620;95.878;
427.120;427.125   Police officers and firefighters.
161.700   Teachers.
427.150   Other pensions needed for support, including IRAs.

PUBLIC BENEFITS
205.220   AFDC; aid to blind, aged and disabled.
341.470   Unemployment compensation.
342.180   Workers' compensation.
427.110   Cooperative life or casualty insurance benefits; fraternal benefit society benefits.
427.150   Crime victims' compensation.

TOOLS OF TRADE
427.010   Farmer's tools, equipment, livestock and poultry up to $3,000.
427.030   Non-farmer's tools up to $300; motor vehicle of mechanic, mechanical or electrical equipment servicer, minister, attorney, physician, surgeon, dentist, veterinarian or chiropractor up to $2,500.
427.040   Library, office equipment, instruments and furnishings of a minister, attorney, physician, surgeon, dentist, veterinarian or chiropractor up to $1,000.

ALIMONY AND CHILD SUPPORT
427.150   Alimony and child support needed for support.

INSURANCE
304.14-300   Life insurance proceeds or cash value if beneficiary is not the insured.
304.14-310   Health or disability benefits.
304.14-320   Group life insurance proceeds.
304.14-330   Annuity contract proceeds up to $350 per month.
304.14-340   Life insurance policy if the beneficiary is a married woman.
304.14-350   Life insurance proceeds if policy prohibits use to pay creditors.

MISCELLANEOUS
362.270   Business partnership property.
Other   Add any applicable Federal Non-Bankruptcy Exemptions.

LOUISIANA

West's LSA Revised Statutes, Title 20, Section 1 (L.R.S.A. §20:1). Ignore volume numbers; look for "section" numbers. Also, be sure to use the volumes marked "Revised Statutes," except for the item marked "Civil 223" under PERSONAL PROPERTY, which will be found in a volume marked "*West's* LSA Civil Code."

HOMESTEAD
20:1   Up to $15,000, but cannot exceed 160 acres on one tract, or 160 acres on more than 1 tract if there is a home on only one of the tracts. Must occupy at time of filing bankruptcy. Spouse or child of deceased owner, or spouse obtaining home in divorce, may claim exemption.(*)

PERSONAL PROPERTY
8:313   Cemetery plot and monuments.

13:3881   Living room, dining room and bedroom furniture; clothing; chinaware, glassware, utensils, and silverware (but not sterling); refrigerator, freezer, stove, washer and dryer; bedding and linens; family portraits; musical instruments; heating and cooling equipment; pressing irons and sewing machine; arms and military accoutrements; poultry, fowl and 1 cow; engagement and wedding rings up to $5,000; and equipment needed for therapy. Also, property of a minor child (also cite as "Civil 223").

WAGES
13:3881   Minimum of 75% of earned but unpaid wages. Judge may approve more for low income debtor.

PENSIONS
13:3881   ERISA-qualified benefit contributions, if deposited more than 1 year before filing.

20:33   Gratuitous payments to employee or heirs, whenever paid.

PUBLIC BENEFITS
23:1205   Workers' compensation.

23:1693   Unemployment compensation.

46:111   AFDC; aid to blind, aged and disabled.

46:1811   Crime victims' compensation.

TOOLS OF TRADE
13:3881   Tools, books, instruments, non-luxury car, pickup truck (up to 3 tons), and utility trailer needed for work.

INSURANCE
22:558   Fraternal benefit society benefits.

22:646   Health, accident or disability proceeds, dividends, interest, loan, cash or surrender value.

22:647   Life insurance proceeds, dividends, interest, loan, cash or surrender value, if policy issued within 9 months of filing, up to $35,000.

22:649   Group insurance policies or proceeds.

MISCELLANEOUS
Other   Add any applicable Federal Non-Bankruptcy Exemptions.

MAINE

Maine Revised Statutes Annotated, Title 14, Section 4422 (14 M.R.S.A. §4422). Ignore volume numbers; look for "title" numbers.

HOMESTEAD (**)
14-4422 $12,500 (up to $60,000 if over 60 or disabled). Includes co-op and property owned by the debtor but used as a residence by a dependent of the debtor. Proceeds for 6 months (must be reinvested in new homestead within 6 months).

PERSONAL PROPERTY
9-A-5-103   Balance due on repossessed goods, provided total amount financed is not more than $2,000.

14-4422   Motor vehicle up to $2,500; cooking stove; furnaces and stoves for heat; food to last 6 months; fuel not to exceed 5 tons of coal, 1,000 gallons of oil, or 10 cords of wood; health aids; 1 wedding ring & 1 engagement ring; other jewelry up to $750; up to $200 per item for each of the following: household goods & furnishings, clothing, appliances, books, animals, crops, and musical instruments; lost earnings payments needed for support; feed, seed, fertilizer, tools and equipment to raise and harvest food for 1 season; wrongful death recoveries needed for support; personal injury recoveries up to $12,500, not including pain and suffering; $400 of any property. Burial plot for the debtor or a dependent of the debtor, in lieu of homestead exemption.

37-B-262   Military arms, clothes and equipment.

PENSIONS
3-703   Legislators.
4-1203   Judges.
5-17054   State employees.
14-4422   ERISA-qualified benefits.

PUBLIC BENEFITS
14-4422   Unemployment compensation, veterans' benefits, social security, and crime victims' compensation.
22-3753   AFDC
39-67   Workers' compensation.

TOOLS OF TRADE
14-4422   Books, materials and stock up to $5,000; 1 of each type of farm implement necessary to raise and harvest crops; 1 boat not to exceed 5 tons used in commercial fishing.

ALIMONY AND CHILD SUPPORT
14-4422   Alimony and child support needed for support.

INSURANCE
14-4422   Unmatured life insurance policy; life insurance policy, dividends, interest, or loan value for person you depended upon up to $4,000.
24-A-2428   Life, annuity, accident or endowment policy, proceeds, dividends, interest, loan, cash or surrender value.
24-A-2429   Disability or health insurance proceeds, dividends, interest, loan, cash or surrender value.
24-A-2430   Group life or health policy or proceeds.
24-A-2431   Annuity proceeds up to $450 per month.
24-A-4118   Fraternal benefit society benefits.

MISCELLANEOUS
14-4422   Unused homestead to $6,000 total for tools of trade, personal injury recoveries, or household goods & furnishings, clothing, appliances, books, animals, crops, and musical instruments.
31-305   Business partnership property.
Other   Add any applicable Federal Non-Bankruptcy Exemptions.

MARYLAND

References with numbers only are to Annotated Code of Maryland, Article 23, Section 164 (A.C.M. §23-164). Other references are to specific volumes, which have the title on the book. Example: "A.C.M. Courts and Judicial Procedure §11-504 (Ct. & Jud. Proc. 11-504)," or "A.C.M. Corporations §9-502 (Corp. 9-502)."

HOMESTEAD

Tenancies by the entirety to unlimited amount as to debts of one spouse [In re *Sefren*, 41 B.R. 747 (D. Md. 1984)].

PERSONAL PROPERTY

Ct.&Jud.Proc.11-504	Clothing, household goods & furnishings, appliances, books and pets up to $500 total; health aids; cash or property up to $3,000; lost future earnings recoveries.
23-164	Burial plot.

WAGES

Comm.15-601.1	Earned but unpaid wages are exempt as follows: in Kent, Caroline and Queen Anne's of Worcester counties, the greater of 75% of actual wages or 30% of the federal minimum wage; in all other counties, the greater of 75% or $145 per week.

PENSIONS

73B-17;73B-125	State employees.
73B-49	Deceased Baltimore police officers, but only as to benefits accruing.
73B-96;73B-152	Teachers.
88B-60	State police.
Ct. & Jud. Proc. 11-504	ERISA-qualified benefits, except IRAs.

PUBLIC BENEFITS

26A-13	Crime victims' compensation.
88A-73	AFDC; general assistance.
95A-16	Unemployment compensation.
101-50	Workers' compensation.

TOOLS OF TRADE

Ct.&Jud.Proc.11-504	Tools, books, instruments, appliances and clothing needed for work (but can't include car), up to $2,500.

INSURANCE

48A-328,Estates and Trusts 8-115	Fraternal benefit society benefits.
48A-385,Estates and Trusts 8-115	Life insurance or annuity contract proceeds, dividends, interest, loan, cash or surrender value if beneficiary is a dependent of the insured.
Comm.15-601.1	Medical benefits deducted from wages.
Ct.&Jud.Proc.11-504	Disability or health benefits.

MISCELLANEOUS

Corp. 9-502	Business partnership property.
Other	Add any applicable Federal Non-Bankruptcy Exemptions.

MASSACHUSETTS

Annotated Laws of Massachusetts, Chapter 188, Section 1 (A.L.M. §188-1). Compare Federal Bankruptcy Exemptions.

HOMESTEAD

188-1; 188-1A $100,000; if over 65 or disabled then $200,000. Some tenancies by the entirety are exempt without limit. Must record homestead declaration before filing bankruptcy. Must occupy or intend to occupy the property at the time of filing for bankruptcy. Spouse or child of deceased owner may claim the exemption.(*)

209-1 Tenancies by the entirety exempt as against debts for non-necessities.

PERSONAL PROPERTY

79-6A Moving expenses for eminent domain (that is, if the government took your property).

235-34 Motor vehicle up to $750; furniture up to $3,000; clothing needed; beds and bedding; heating unit; books up to $200 total; cash up to $200 per month for rent, in lieu of homestead; cash for fuel, heat, water or electricity up to $75 per month; bank deposits to $125; cash for food or food to $300; sewing machine to $200; burial plots and tombs; church pew; 2 cows, 2 swine, 12 sheep and 4 tons of hay. Co-op shares up to $100.

246-28A Bank, credit union or trust company deposits up to $500 total.

WAGES

246-28 Earned but unpaid wages up to $125 per week.

PENSIONS

32-19 Public employees.
32-41 Private retirement benefits.
168-41; 168-44 Savings bank employees.
235-34A; 246-28 ERISA-qualified benefits.

PUBLIC BENEFITS

115-5 Veterans' benefits.
118-10 AFDC
151A-36 Unemployment compensation.
152-47 Workers' compensation.
235-34 Aid to aged and disabled.

TOOLS OF TRADE

235-34 Tools, implements and fixtures up to $500 total; materials you designed and procured up to $500; boats, nets and fishing tackle of fisherman up to $500; arms, uniforms and accoutrements you are required to keep.

INSURANCE

175-110A Disability benefits up to $400 per week.
175-119A Life insurance proceeds if policy prohibits use to pay creditors.
175-125 Life insurance annuity contract which states it is exempt; life or endowment policy, proceeds, dividends, interest, loan, cash or surrender value.
175-126 Life insurance policy if beneficiary is a married woman.
175-132C Group annuity policy or proceeds.
175-135 Group life insurance policy.
175F-15 Medical malpractice self-insurance.
176-22 Fraternal benefit society benefits.

MISCELLANEOUS

108A-25 Business partnership property.
Other Add any applicable Federal Non-Bankruptcy Exemptions.

MICHIGAN

Michigan Compiled Laws Annotated, Section 600.6023. (M.C.L.A. §600.6023). (In addition to the Michigan Compiled Laws, there are also the Michigan Statutes Annotated, or "M.S.A." If you wish to look up these laws but can only find the M.S.A., there is a cross-reference to the M.C.LA. number in the M.S.A. itself.) Compare Federal Bankruptcy Exemptions.

HOMESTEAD

Real property, including condominium, up to $3,500; but not to exceed 1 lot in a city, town or village, or 40 acres elsewhere. Tenancies by the entirety are exempt without limit as to debts of one spouse [*SNB Bank & Trust v. Kensey*, 378 NW2d 594 (Mich. App. 1985)]. Spouse or child of a deceased owner may claim the exemption.

PERSONAL PROPERTY

128.112	Burial plots.
600.6023	Clothing; household goods, furniture, appliances, utensils and books up to $1,000 total; food and fuel to last 6 months if head of household; building and loan association shares up to $1,000 par value, in lieu of homestead exemption; family pictures; church pew, slip or seat; 2 cows, 5 swine, 10 sheep, 5 roosters, 100 hens, and hay and grain to last 6 months if head of household.

WAGES

600.5311	60% of earned but unpaid wages for head of household; 40% for others; subject to following minimums: $15 per week plus $2 per week for each dependent other than spouse for head of household; $10 per week for others.

PENSIONS

38.40	State employees.		38.1057	Legislators.
38.559	Police officers and firefighters.		38.1346	Public school employees.
38.826	Judges.		600.6023	IRAs, to extent tax-deferred; ERISA-qualified benefits.
38.927	Probate judges.			

PUBLIC BENEFITS

18.362	Crime victims' compensation.
35.926	Veterans' benefits for WWII veterans.
35.977	Korean War veterans' benefits.
35.1027	Vietnam veterans' benefits.
330.1158a	AFDC.
400.63	Social welfare benefits.
418.821	Workers' compensation.
421.30	Unemployment compensation.

TOOLS OF TRADE

600.6023	Tools, implements, materials, stock, apparatus, motor vehicle, horse, team and harness up to $1,000 total; arms and accoutrements you are required to keep.

INSURANCE

500.2207	Life insurance proceeds, dividends, interest, loan, cash or surrender value; life or endowment proceeds if beneficiary is spouse or child of insured.
500.2209	Life insurance proceeds up to $300 per year if the beneficiary is a married woman or a husband.
500.4054	Life, annuity or endowment proceeds if policy or contract prohibits use to pay creditors.
500.8046	Fraternal benefit society benefits.
600.6023	Disability, mutual life or health benefits.

MISCELLANEOUS

449.25	Business partnership property
Other	Add any applicable Federal Non-Bankruptcy Exemptions.

MINNESOTA

Minnesota Statutes Annotated, Section 510.01 (M.S.A. §510.01). Ignore volume numbers; look for "section" numbers. Be sure to see Cumulative Annual Pocket Part for current limitation amounts. NOTE: Some courts have held "unlimited" exemptions invalid as state constitution only allows for "reasonable" exemptions. In re *Tveten*, 402 NW2d 551 (Minn. 1987). NOTE: Amounts are adjusted periodically. The next adjustment is due 4/30/98 to become effective on 7/1/98. Compare Federal Bankruptcy Exemptions.

HOMESTEAD
510.01;510.02; 550.37   Real property, mobile or manufacturer home up to $200,000 ($500,000 if used primarily for agriculture), but cannot exceed 1/2 acre in "the laid out or platted portion of" a city or 160 acres elsewhere. Sale and insurance proceeds for 1 year.

PERSONAL PROPERTY
550.37   Motor vehicle up to $3,400 ($34,000 if modified for disability at a cost of at least $2,550); clothing, including watch; furniture, appliances, radio, TV and phonographs up to $7,650 total; food and utensils; books and musical instruments; burial plot; church pew or seat; proceeds for damaged or destroyed exempt property; personal injury lost earnings and wrongful death recoveries.

WAGES
550.37   Wages deposited into bank accounts for 20 days after deposit; earned but unpaid wages paid within 6 months of returning to work if you previously received welfare; wages of released inmates paid received within 6 months of release.

571.55   Minimum of 75% of earned but unpaid wages. Judge may approve more for low income debtor.

550.37   Earnings of a minor child.

PENSIONS
181B.16	Private retirement benefits accruing.	550.37	ERISA-qualified benefits, including IRAs, needed for support, up to $51,000 present value.
352.15	State employees.		
352B.071	State troopers.		
353.15	Public employees.		
354.10;354A.11	Teachers.		

PUBLIC BENEFITS
176.175   Workers' compensation.

268.17   Unemployment compensation.

550.37   AFDC, supplemental security income (SSI), general assistance, supplemental assistance.

550.38   Veterans' benefits.

611A.60   Crime victims' compensation.

TOOLS OF TRADE
550.37   Tools, library, furniture, machines, instruments, implements and stock in trade up to $8,500; Farm machines, implements, livestock, produce and crops of farmers up to $13,000. (Total of these cannot exceed $13,000.) Teaching materials of a school teacher, including books and chemical apparatus, of unlimited value and not subject to $13,000 limit.

INSURANCE
61A.04   Life insurance proceeds if policy prohibits use to pay creditors.

61A.12   Life insurance or endowment proceeds, dividends, interest, loan, cash or surrender value if the insured is not the beneficiary.

64B.18   Fraternal benefit society benefits.

550.37   Life insurance proceeds if beneficiary is spouse or child, up to $34,000 plus additional $8,500 per dependent; unmatured life insurance contract dividends, interest, loan, cash or surrender value if insured is the debtor or someone the debtor depends upon, up to $6,800; police, fire or beneficiary association benefits.

550.39   Accident or disability proceeds.

MISCELLANEOUS
323.24   Business partnership property.

Other   Add any applicable Federal Non-Bankruptcy Exemptions.

MISSISSIPPI

Mississippi Code 1972 Annotated, Title 85, Section 85-3-21 (M.C. §85-3-21).

HOMESTEAD
85-3-21 $75,000, but cannot exceed 160 acres. Must occupy at time of filing bankruptcy, unless you are widowed or over 60 and married or widowed. Sale proceeds are also exempt. 85-3-23.

PERSONAL PROPERTY
85-3-1   Tangible personal property of any kind up to $10,000; proceeds from exempt property.

85-3-17   Personal injury judgments up to $10,000.

WAGES
85-3-4   Earned but unpaid wages owed for 30 days, 75% after 30 days.

PENSIONS
21-29-257   Police officers and firefighters.

25-11-129   Public employees retirement and disability benefits.

25-11-201-23   Teachers.

25-13-31   Highway patrol officers.

25-14-5   State employees.

71-1-43   Private retirement benefits.

85-3-1   IRAs, Keoghs, and ERISA-qualified benefits, if deposited more than 1 year before filing.

PUBLIC BENEFITS
25-11-129   Social security.

43-3-71   Assistance to blind.

43-9-19   Assistance to aged.

43-29-15   Assistance to disabled.

71-3-43   Workers' compensation.

71-5-539   Unemployment compensation.

99-41-23   Crime victims' compensation.

INSURANCE
83-7-5   Life insurance proceeds if policy prohibits use to pay creditors.

83-29-39   Fraternal benefit society benefits.

85-3-1   Disability benefits.

85-3-11   Life insurance policy or proceeds up to $50,000.

85-3-13   Life insurance proceeds if beneficiary is the decedent's estate, up to $5,000.

85-3-23   Homeowners' insurance proceeds up to $75,000.

MISCELLANEOUS
79-12-49   Business partnership property.

Other   Add any applicable Federal Non-Bankruptcy Exemptions.

MISSOURI

Vernon's Annotated Missouri Statutes, Chapter 513, Section 513.430 (A.M.S. §513.430). Ignore volume numbers; look for "section" numbers.

HOMESTEAD
513.430;
513.475   Real property up to $8,000, or mobile home up to $1,000. Tenancies by the entirety are exempt without limit as to debts of one spouse [In re *Anderson*, 12 B.R. 483 (W.D. Mo. 1981)].(*)

PERSONAL PROPERTY
214.190   Burial grounds up to $100 or 1 acre.

513.430   Motor vehicle up to $1,000; clothing, household goods, appliances, furnishings, books, animals, musical instruments and crops up to $1,000 total; health aids; jewelry up to $500; wrongful death recoveries for a person you depended upon.

513.430;
513.440   Any property up to $1,250 plus $250 per child for head of family; up to $400 for others.

Other   Personal injury causes of action. Refer to as: "In re *Mitchell*, 73 B.R. 93".

WAGES
513.470   Wages of a servant or common laborer up to $90.

525.030   Minimum of 75% of earned but unpaid wages. Judge may approve more for low income debtor. 90% for head of family.

PENSIONS
70.695   Public officers and employees.
71.207   Employees of cities with more than 100,000 population.
86.190;86.353; 86.493;86.780   Police department employees.
87.090;87.365; 87.485   Firefighters.
104.250   Highway and transportation employees.
104.540   State employees.
169.090   Teachers.
513.430   ERISA-qualified benefits needed for support; life insurance dividends, loan value, or interest, up to $5,000, if bought more than 6 months before filing.

PUBLIC BENEFITS
287.260   Workers' compensation.
288.380; 513.430   Unemployment compensation.
513.430   Social security, veterans' benefits, and AFDC.

TOOLS OF TRADE
513.430   Tools, books and implements to $2,000.

ALIMONY AND CHILD SUPPORT
513.430   Alimony and child support up to $500 per month.

INSURANCE
376.530; 376.560   Life insurance proceeds if policy owned by woman insuring her husband.

376.550   Life insurance proceeds if policy owned by an unmarried woman and beneficiary is her father or brother.

377.090   Fraternal benefit society benefits, up to $5,000, if bought more than 6 months before filing.

377.330   Assessment or stipulated premium proceeds.

513.430   Death, disability or illness benefits needed for support; unmatured life insurance policy.

MISCELLANEOUS
358.250   Business partnership property.
Other   Add any applicable Federal Non-Bankruptcy Exemptions.

MONTANA

Montana Code Annotated, Title 70, Chapter 32, Section 70-32-101 (M.C.A. §70-32-101). Ignore volume numbers; look for "title" numbers.

HOMESTEAD
70-32-101; 70-32-104; 70-32-201;
70-32-216 Real property or mobile home up to $40,000. Must occupy at time of filing for bankruptcy, and must record a homestead declaration before filing. Proceeds for 18 months.

PERSONAL PROPERTY
25-13-608 Health aids; burial plot.
25-13-609 Motor vehicle up to $1,200; clothing, household goods and furnishings, appliances, jewelry, books, animals and feed, musical instruments, firearms, sporting goods, and crops up to $600 per item and $4,500 total.
25-13-610 Proceeds for damaged or lost exempt property for 6 months after receipt.
35-15-404 Cooperative association shares up to $500 value.

WAGES
25-13-614 Minimum of 75% of earned but unpaid wages. Judge may approve more for low income debtor.

PENSIONS
19-3-105	Public employees.	
19-4-706	Teachers.	
19-5-704	Judges.	
19-6-705	Highway patrol officers.	
19-7-705	Sheriffs.	
19-8-805	Game wardens.	

19-9-1006;19-10-504 Police officers.
19-11-612;19-13-1004 Firefighters.
19-21-212 University system employees.
31-2-106 ERISA-qualified benefits in excess of 15% of annual income, if deposited at least 1 year before filing.

PUBLIC BENEFITS
25-13-608 Social security, veterans', & local public assistance benefits.
39-71-743 Workers' compensation.
39-73-110 Silicosis benefits.
39-51-3105 Unemployment compensation.
53-2-607 AFDC, aid to aged and disabled, vocational rehabilitation to the blind, subsidized adoption payments.
53-9-129 Crime victims' compensation.

TOOLS OF TRADE
25-13-609 Tools, books and instruments of trade up to $3,000.
25-13-613 Arms, uniforms and accoutrements needed to carry out government functions.

ALIMONY AND CHILD SUPPORT
25-13-608 Alimony and child support.

INSURANCE
25-13-608; 33-15-513 Disability or illness proceeds, benefits, dividends, interest, loan, cash or surrender value, and medical or hospital benefits.
25-13-609 Unmatured life insurance contracts up to $4,000.
33-7-511 Fraternal benefit society benefits.
33-15-511 Life insurance proceeds, dividends, interest, loan, cash or surrender value.
33-15-512 Group life insurance policy or proceeds.
33-15-514 Annuity contract proceeds up to $350 per month.
33-20-120 Life insurance proceeds if policy prohibits use to pay creditors.
80-2-245 Hail insurance benefits.

MISCELLANEOUS
35-10-502 Business partnership property.
Other Add any applicable Federal Non-Bankruptcy Exemptions.

NEBRASKA

Revised Statutes of Nebraska, Chapter 40, Section 40-101 (R.S.N. §40-101). Ignore volume numbers; look for "chapter" numbers.

HOMESTEAD
40-101 $10,000, but cannot exceed 2 lots in a city or 160 acres elsewhere. Sale proceeds are exempt for 6 months after sale.

PERSONAL PROPERTY
12-511   Perpetual care funds.
12-517   Burial plot.
12-605   Tombs, crypts, lots, niches and vaults.
25-1552 $2,500 of any property except wages, in lieu of homestead.
25-1556   Personal possessions; clothing needed; furniture and kitchen utensils up to $1,500; food and fuel to last 6 months.
25-1563   Recovery for personal injuries.

WAGES
25-1558   Minimum of 85% of earned but unpaid wages or pension payments for head of family; 75% for others. Judge may approve more for low income debtor.

PENSIONS
23-2322   County employees.
25-1559   Military disability benefits up to $2,000.
25-1563   ERISA-qualified benefits needed for support.
79-1060;
79-1552   School employees.
84-1324   State employees.

PUBLIC BENEFITS
48-149   Workers' compensation.
48-647   Unemployment compensation.
68-1013   AFDC; aid to blind, aged and disabled.

TOOLS OF TRADE
25-1556   Tools or equipment up to $1,500. (**)

INSURANCE
44-371   Life insurance or annuity contract proceeds up to $10,000 loan value.
44-754   Disability benefits to $200 per month.
44-1089   Fraternal benefit society benefits up to loan value of $10,000.

MISCELLANEOUS
67-325   Business partnership property.
Other   Add any applicable Federal Non-Bankruptcy Exemptions.

NEVADA

Nevada Revised Statutes Annotated, Chapter 21, Section 21.090 (N.R.S.A. §21.090(m)). Ignore volume numbers; look for "chapter" numbers.

HOMESTEAD (*)

21.090(m); 115.010   Real property or mobile home up to $125,000. Must record a homestead declaration before filing for bankruptcy (115.020).

PERSONAL PROPERTY

21.090   Motor vehicle up to $1,500 (no limit if equipped for the disabled); household goods, furniture, home and yard equipment up to $3,000 total; books up to $1,500 total; pictures and keepsakes; health aids; 1 gun.

21.100   Metal-bearing ores, geological specimens, paleontological remains or art curiosities (must be arranged, classified, catalogued, and numbered in reference books).

452.550   Burial plot purchase money held in trust.

689.700   Funeral service contract money held in trust.

WAGES

21.090   Minimum of 75% of earned but unpaid wages. Judge may approve more for low income debtor.

PENSIONS

286.670   Public employees.

PUBLIC BENEFITS

422.291   AFDC; aid to blind, aged and disabled.

612.710   Unemployment compensation.

615.270   Vocational rehabilitation benefits.

616.550   Industrial insurance (worker's compensation).

TOOLS OF TRADE

21.090   Tools, materials, library, equipment and supplies up to $4,500; farm trucks, equipment, tools, stock and seed up to $4,500; cabin or dwelling of a miner or prospector, cars, implements and appliances for mining and a mining claim you work up to $4,500; arms, uniforms and accoutrements you are required to keep.

INSURANCE

21.090   Life insurance policy or proceeds if premiums don't exceed $1,000 per year.

687B.260   Life insurance proceeds if you are not insured.

687B.270   Health insurance proceeds, dividends, interest, loan, cash or surrender value.

687B.280   Group life or health policy or proceeds.

687B.290   Annuity contract proceeds up to $350 per month.

695A.220   Fraternal benefit society benefits.

MISCELLANEOUS

87.250   Business partnership property.

Other   Add any applicable Federal Non-Bankruptcy Exemptions.

NEW HAMPSHIRE

New Hampshire Revised Statutes Annotated, Chapter 480, Section 480:1 (N.H.R.S.A. §480:1). Ignore "title" numbers; look for "chapter" numbers.

HOMESTEAD
480:1 Real property, or manufactured home if you own the land, up to $30,000.

PERSONAL PROPERTY
511:2 (1) clothing; (2) beds, bedsteads, and bedding; (3) furniture up to $3,500; (4) one refrigerator, cooking stove, and heating stove, and utensils for each; (5) sewing machine; (6) provisions and fuel up to $400; (7) books up to $800; (8) 1 hog and 1 pig, or pork if already slaughtered; (9) 6 sheep and their fleeces; (10) 1 cow, 1 yoke of oxen or a horse (if needed for farming, etc.), and hay up to 4 tons; (11) domestic fowls up to $300; (12) church pew; (13) automobile up to $4,000; (14) jewelry up to $500; and (15) any property up to $1,000. Also up to $7,000 in any property for any unused amounts allowed for items (3), (6), (7), (13), (14), and tools of trade.

512:21 Proceeds for lost or destroyed exempt property.

WAGES
512:21 Earned but unpaid wages of debtor and spouse (Judge determines amount exempt based on percent of federal minimum wage, so claim all); jury and witness fees; wages of a minor child.

PENSIONS
100A:26	Public employees.	103:18	Police officers.
102:23	Firefighters.	512:21	Federally created pensions accruing.

PUBLIC BENEFITS
167:25 AFDC; aid to blind, aged and disabled.
281A:52 Workers' compensation.
282A:159 Unemployment compensation.

TOOLS OF TRADE
511:2 Tools of trade up to $5,000; arms, uniforms and equipment of a military member; 1 yoke of oxen or horse needed for farming or teaming.

ALIMONY AND CHILD SUPPORT
161C:11 Child support only.

INSURANCE
402:69 Firefighters' aid insurance.
408:1 Life insurance or endowment proceeds if beneficiary is a married woman.
408:2 Life insurance or endowment proceeds if you are not the insured.
418:24 Fraternal benefit society benefits.
512:21 Homeowners' insurance proceeds up to $5,000.

MISCELLANEOUS
304A:25 Business partnership property.
Other   Add any applicable Federal Non-Bankruptcy Exemptions.

NEW JERSEY

New Jersey Statutes Annotated, Title 2A, Chapter 17, Section 2A-17-19 (N.J.S.A. §2A:17-19). The spine of these volumes will be marked "NJSA." Compare Federal Bankruptcy Exemptions.

PERSONAL PROPERTY
2A:17-19	Clothing; goods, personal property and stock or interest in corporations up to $1,000 total.
2A:26-4	Household good and furniture up to $1,000.
8A:5-10	Burial plots.

WAGES
2A:17-56	90% of earned but unpaid wages if your income is less than $7,500; otherwise judge may exempt less.
38A:4-8	Military personnel wages and allowances.

PENSIONS
A:057.6	Civil defense workers.
18A:66-51	Teachers.
18A:66-116	School district employees.
43:6A-41	Judges.
43:7-13	Prison employees.
43:8A-20	Alcohol beverage control officers.
43:10-57; 43:10-105	County employees.
43-13-9	ERISA-qualified benefits.
43:13-44	Municipal employees.
43:15A-55	Public employees.
43:16-7; 43:16A-17	Police officers, firefighters and traffic officers.
43:18-12	City boards of health employees.
43:19-17	Street and water department employees.
53:5A-45	State police.

PUBLIC BENEFITS
34:15-29	Workers' compensation.
43:21-53	Unemployment compensation.
44:7-35	Old-age, permanent disability assistance.
52:4B-30	Crime victims' compensation.

INSURANCE
A:9-57.6	Civil defense workers' disability, death, medical or hospital benefits.
17:18-12; 17B:24-8	Health and disability benefits.
17:44A-19	Fraternal benefit society benefits.
17B:24-6	Life insurance proceeds, dividends, interest, loan, cash or surrender value, if you are not the insured.
17B:24-7	Annuity contract proceeds up to $500 per month.
17B:24-9	Group life or health policy or proceeds.
17B:24-10	Life insurance proceeds if policy prohibits use to pay creditors.
38A:4-8	Military member disability or death benefits.

MISCELLANEOUS
42:1-25	Business partnership property.
Other	Add any applicable Federal Non-Bankruptcy Exemptions.

NEW MEXICO

New Mexico Statutes 1978 Annotated, Chapter 42, Section 42-10-9 (N.M.S.A. §42-10-9). Ignore volume numbers; look for "chapter" numbers. Compare Federal Bankruptcy Exemptions.

HOMESTEAD (**)
42-10-9 $30,000 only if married, widowed or supporting another person.

PERSONAL PROPERTY
42-10-1   Motor vehicle up to $4,000; $500 of any property.
42-10-1; 42-10-2   Clothing; jewelry up to $2,500; books, furniture, and health equipment.
42-10-10 $2,000 of any property, in lieu of homestead.
48-2-15   Building materials.
53-4-28   Minimum amount of shares needed for membership in cooperative association.
70-4-12   Tools, machinery and materials needed to dig, drill, torpedo, complete, operate or repair an oil line, gas well or pipeline.

WAGES
35-12-7   Minimum of 75% of earned but unpaid wages. Judge may approve more for low income debtor.

PENSIONS
22-11-42   Public school employees.
42-10-1;
42-10-2   Pension or retirement benefits.

PUBLIC BENEFITS
27-2-21   AFDC; general assistance.
31-22-15   Crime victims' compensation paid before July 1, 1993.
51-1-37   Unemployment compensation.
52-1-52   Workers' compensation.
52-3-37   Occupational disease disablement benefits.

TOOLS OF TRADE
42-10-1;
42-10-2 $1,500.

INSURANCE
42-10-3   Life, accident, health or annuity benefits or cash value, if beneficiary is a citizen of New Mexico.
42-10-4   Benevolent association benefits up to $5,000.
42-10-5   Life insurance proceeds.
59A-44-18 Fraternal benefit society benefits.

MISCELLANEOUS
53-10-2   Ownership in an unincorporated association.
54-1-25   Business partnership property.
Other   Add any applicable Federal Non-Bankruptcy Exemptions.

NEW YORK

References of numbers only are to *McKinney's* Consolidated Laws of New York, Civil Practice Law and Rules, Section 5206 (C.P.L.R. §5206). Other references are to "Debtor & Creditor" (D&C); "Estates, Powers & Trusts" (Est, Pow & Tr.); "Insurance" (Insur.); "Retirement & Social Security" (Ret. & Soc. Sec.); "Partnership" (Part.); and "Unconsolidated" (Unc.).

HOMESTEAD
5206   Real property, including mobile home, condominium or coop, up to $10,000.(**)

PERSONAL PROPERTY
5205   Clothing, furniture, refrigerator, TV, radio, sewing machine, security deposits with landlord or utility company, tableware, cooking utensils and crockery, stoves with food and fuel to last 60 days, health aids (including animals with food), church pew or seat, wedding ring, bible, schoolbooks, pictures; books up to $50; burial plot without a structure to 1/4 acre; domestic animals with food to $450; watch to $35; trust fund principal; 90% of trust fund income.

D&C282   Motor vehicle up to $2,400; lost earnings recoveries needed for support; personal injury recoveries up to $7,500, not including pain and suffering; wrongful death recoveries for a person you depended upon for support.

D&C283   IN LIEU OF HOMESTEAD: Cash in the lesser amount of $2,500, or an amount when added to an annuity equals $5,000.

WAGES
5205   90% of earned but unpaid wages received within 60 days of filing for bankruptcy; 90% of earnings from milk sales to milk dealers; 100% for a few militia members.

PENSIONS
5205; D&C 282   ERISA-qualified plans, Keoghs and IRAs needed for support.
Insur. 4607   Public retirement benefits.
Ret. & Soc. Sec. 110   State employees.
Unc. 5711-o   Village police officers.

PUBLIC BENEFITS
D&C282   Unemployment benefits; veterans' benefits; social security; AFDC; aid to blind, aged and disabled; crime victims' compensation; home relief; local public assistance.

TOOLS OF TRADE
5205   Professional furniture, books, instruments, farm machinery, team and food for 60 days, up to $600 total; arms, swords, uniforms, equipment, horse, emblem and medal of a military member.

ALIMONY AND CHILD SUPPORT
D&C282   Alimony and child support needed for support.

INSURANCE
5205   Insurance proceeds for damaged exempt property.
5205; D&C283   Annuity contract benefits up to $5,000, if purchased within 6 months of filing for bankruptcy and not tax-deferred.
Est,Pow&Tr.7-1.5   Life insurance proceeds if policy prohibits use to pay creditors.
Insur.3212   Fraternal benefit society benefits; disability or illness benefits up to $400 per month; life insurance proceeds, dividends, interest, loan, cash or surrender value if beneficiary is not the insured.

MISCELLANEOUS
Part. 51   Business partnership property.
Other   Add any applicable Federal Non-Bankruptcy Exemptions.

NORTH CAROLINA

General Statutes of North Carolina, Chapter 1C, Section 1C-1601 (G.S.N.C. §1C-1601). Ignore volume numbers; look for "chapter" numbers.

HOMESTEAD
1C-1601 Real or personal property used as a residence, including coop, up to $10,000. Tenancies by the entirety exempt without limit as to debts of one spouse [*In re Crouch*, 33 B.R. 271 (E.D. N.C. 1983)].

PERSONAL PROPERTY
1C-1601 Motor vehicle up to $1,500; health aids; clothing, household goods, furnishings, appliances, books, animals, musical instruments and crops up to $3,500 total, plus additional $750 per dependent up to 4 dependents; personal injury and wrongful death recoveries for a person you depended upon; $3,500 of any property, less any amount claimed for homestead or burial plot.

1C-1601 Burial plot up to $10,000, in lieu of homestead.

1C-1601 $3,500 of any property, less any amount claimed for homestead or burial plot.

WAGES
1-362 Earned but unpaid wages received 60 days before filing for bankruptcy.

PENSIONS
58-86-90 Firefighters and rescue squad workers.
120-4.29 Legislators.
128-31 Municipal, city and county employees.
135-9;135-95 Teachers and state employees.
143-166.30 Law enforcement officers.

PUBLIC BENEFITS
15B-17 Crime victims' compensation.
96-17 Unemployment compensation.
97-21 Workers' compensation.
108A-36 AFDC; special adult assistance.
111-18 Aid to blind.

TOOLS OF TRADE
1C-1601 Tools, books and implements of trade up to $750.

INSURANCE
Const.10-5 Life insurance policy if beneficiary is insured spouse or child.
58-58-115 Life insurance proceeds, dividends, interest, loan, cash or surrender value.
58-58-165 Group life insurance policy or proceeds.
58-58-165 Employee group life policy or proceeds.
58-24-85 Fraternal benefit society benefits.

MISCELLANEOUS
59-55 Business partnership property.
Other Add any applicable Federal Non-Bankruptcy Exemptions.

NORTH DAKOTA

North Dakota Century Code Annotated, Title 28, Chapter 28-22, Section 28-22-02 (N.D.C.C. §28-22-02). Ignore volume numbers; look for "title" numbers.

HOMESTEAD
28-22-02; 47-18-01   Real property, mobile home or house trailer up to $80,000.

PERSONAL PROPERTY
The following list applies to all debtors:

28-22-02   Clothing; fuel to last 1 year; bible; books up to $100; pictures; church pew; burial plots; crops or grain raised on the debtor's tract of land, limited to 1 tract of 160 acres.

28-22-03.1   Motor vehicle up to $1,200; personal injury recoveries not including pain and suffering, up to $7,500; wrongful death recoveries up to $7,500.

28-22-03.1   IN LIEU OF HOMESTEAD: cash to $7,500.

The following list applies to the head of household, not claiming crops or grain:

28-22-03 $5,000 of any personal property; OR

28-22-04   Furniture and bedding up to $1,000; books and musical instruments up to $1,500; tools and library of a professional up to $1,000; tools of a mechanic and stock in trade up to $1,000; and farm implements and livestock up to $4,500.

The following list applied to a non-head of household not claiming crops:

28-22-05 $2,500 of any personal property.

WAGES
32-09.1-.03   Minimum of 75% of earned but unpaid wages. Judge may approve more for low income debtor.

PENSIONS
28-22-03.1   Disabled veterans' benefits (does not include military retirement pay); annuities, pensions, IRAs, Keoghs, simplified employee plans (together with the insurance exemption under this section total may not exceed $200,000, although no limit if needed for support).

28-22-19   Public employees.

PUBLIC BENEFITS
28-22-03.1   Social security.

28-22-19   AFDC; crime victims' compensation.

37-25-07   Vietnam veterans' adjustment compensation.

52-06-30   Unemployment compensation.

65-05-29   Workers' compensation.

TOOLS OF TRADE
        See personal property section.

INSURANCE
26.1-15.1-18; 26.1-33-40   Fraternal benefit society benefits.

26.1-33-40   Life insurance proceeds payable to the decedent's estate.

28-22-03.1   Life insurance surrender value to $100,000 per policy if beneficiary is relative of the insured and policy was owned for more than 1 year before filing for bankruptcy. Together with pension exemption in this section, total cannot exceed $200,000, or $100,000 per plan, but no limit if needed for support.

MISCELLANEOUS
45-08-02   Business partnership property.

Other   Add any applicable Federal Non-Bankruptcy Exemptions.

OHIO

Page's Ohio Revised Code, Title 23, Section 2329.66 (O.R.C. §2329.66).

HOMESTEAD
2329.66   Real or personal property used as a residence up to $5,000. Tenancies by the entirety are exempt without limit as to debts of one spouse [*In re Thomas*, 14 B.R. 423 (N.D. Ohio 1981)].

PERSONAL PROPERTY
517.09;2329.66 Burial plot.

2329.66   (1) motor vehicle up to $1,000; (2) clothing, beds and bedding up to $200 per item; (3) cooking unit and refrigerator up to $300 each; (4) cash, bank and security deposits, tax refund and money due within 90 days up to $400 total (may include earnings not otherwise exempt); (5) household goods, furnishings, appliances, jewelry, books, animals, musical instruments, firearms, hunting and fishing equipment and crops up to $200 per item (see LIMIT below); (6) jewelry, up to $400 for one piece and up to $200 for each other piece (see LIMIT below); (7) health aids; (8) wrongful death recoveries for person you depended upon for support; (9) compensation for lost future earnings needed for support; (10) personal injury recoveries not including pain and suffering up to $5,000; and (11) $400 of any property. LIMIT: If homestead is not claimed, items under (5) and (6) may not exceed $2,000 total ($1,500 if homestead is claimed). **NOTE:** Section 2329.66 is relatively detailed and complex, so be sure to read it.

WAGES
2329.66   Minimum of 75% of earned but unpaid wages. Judge may approve more for low income debtor.

PENSIONS
145.56   Public employees.
146.13   Volunteer firefighters' dependents.
742.47   Police officers and firefighters.
2329.66   Police officers' and firefighters' death benefits; ERISA-qualified benefits, IRAs and Keoghs needed for support.
3307.71;3309.66   Public school employees.
5505.22   State highway patrol employees.

PUBLIC BENEFITS
2329.66;4123.67   Workers' compensation.
2329.66;4141.32   Unemployment compensation.
2329.66;5107.12   AFDC.

2329.66; 5115.07   Disability assistance.
2743.66   Crime victims' compensation.
3304.19   Vocational rehabilitation benefits.

TOOLS OF TRADE
147.04   Seal and official register of a notary public.
2329.66   Tools, books, and implements of trade up to $750.

ALIMONY AND CHILD SUPPORT
2329.66   Alimony and child support needed for support.

INSURANCE
2329.63;2329.66   Benevolent society benefits to $5,000.
2329.66;3917.05   Group life insurance policy or proceeds.
2329.66;3921.18   Fraternal benefit society benefits.
2329.66;3923.19   Disability benefits to $600 per month.
3911.10   Life, endowment or annuity contract dividends, interest, loan, cash or surrender value for your spouse, child or other dependent.
3911.12   Life insurance proceeds for spouse.
3911.14   Life insurance proceeds if policy prohibits use to pay creditors.

MISCELLANEOUS
1775.24; 2329.66 Business partnership property.
Other   Add any applicable Federal Non-Bankruptcy Exemptions.

OKLAHOMA

Oklahoma Statutes Annotated. Title 31, Section 2 (31 O.S.A. §2).

HOMESTEAD
31-2   Real property or manufactured home to unlimited value, but cannot exceed 1/4 acre. If over 1/4 acre, you may claim up to $5,000 on 1 acre in a city, town or village, or $5,000 on 160 acres elsewhere. You do not need to occupy the home as long as you don't acquire another.

PERSONAL PROPERTY
8-7   Burial plots.
31-1   Motor vehicle up to $3,000; clothing up to $4,000; furniture, books, portraits, pictures, gun and health aids; food to last 1 year; 2 bridles and 2 saddles; 100 chickens, 20 sheep, 10 hogs, 5 cows and calves under 6 months, 2 horses and forage for livestock to last 1 year; personal injury, workers' compensation and wrongful death recoveries (not to include punitive damages) up to $50,000 total.

WAGES
12-1171.1;31-1   75% of wages earned within 90 days prior to filing bankruptcy. Judge may approve more if you can show hardship.

PENSIONS
11-49-126	Firefighters.	31-7	Disabled veterans.
11-50-124	Police officers.	47-2-303.3	Law enforcement employees.
19-959	County employees.	60-328	Tax exempt benefits.
31-1	ERISA-qualified benefits.	70-17-109	Teachers.

PUBLIC BENEFITS
21-142.13   Crime victims' compensation.
40-2-303   Unemployment compensation.
56-173   AFDC; social security.
85-48   Workers' compensation.

TOOLS OF TRADE
31-1   Tools, books, apparatus of trade, and husbandry implements to farm homestead, up to $5,000 total.

ALIMONY AND CHILD SUPPORT
31-1   Alimony and child support.

INSURANCE
36-2410   Assessment or mutual benefits.
36-2510   Limited stock insurance benefits.
36-2720   Fraternal benefit society benefits.
36-3631   Life insurance policy or proceeds if you are not the insured.
36-3632   Group life insurance policy or proceeds if you are not the insured.
36-6125   Funeral benefits if pre-paid and placed in trust.

MISCELLANEOUS
54-225   Business partnership property.
Other   Add any applicable Federal Non-Bankruptcy Exemptions.

OREGON

Oregon Revised Statutes Annotated, Chapter 23, Section 23.164 (O.R.S. §23.164). Ignore volume numbers; look for "chapter" numbers. All exemptions may be doubled by husband and wife [*In re Wilson*, 22 B.R. 146 (D. Ore. 1982)].

HOMESTEAD
23.164;23.250 Real property, houseboat, or mobile home on land you own up to $25,000 ($33,000 if joint owners). Mobile home on land you don't own, $23,000 ($30,000 if joint). Property may not exceed 1 block in a city or town, or 160 acres elsewhere. Must occupy or intend to at time of filing. Sale proceeds exempt 1 year if plan to purchase another home.

PERSONAL PROPERTY
23.160   Motor vehicle to $1,700(**); clothing, jewelry, personal items to $1,800 total(**); household items, furniture, utensils, TVs and radios to $3,000 total; health aids; cash for sold exempt property; books, pictures & musical instruments to $600 total(**); food & fuel to last 60 days if debtor is householder; domestic animals & poultry with food to last 60 days to $1,000; lost earnings payments for debtor or someone debtor depended upon needed for support(**); personal injury recoveries (not pain and suffering) to $7,500(**); $400 of any personal property (can't be used to increase an existing exemption).
23.166   Bank deposits up to $7,500, and cash for sold exempt items.
23.200   Pistol; rifle or shotgun if owned by person over the age of 16, up to $1,000.
65.870   Burial plot.

WAGES
23.185   Minimum of 75% of earned but unpaid wages. Judge may approve more for low income debtor.
292.070   Wages withheld in a state employee's bond saving account.

PENSIONS
23.170   Federal, state or local government employees. ERISA-qualified benefits, if deposited at least 1 year before filing (IRAs, but not Keoghs).
237.201   Public officers and employees.
239.261   School district employees.

PUBLIC BENEFITS
23.160;147.325 Crime victims' compensation (**).
344.580   Vocational rehabilitation.
401.405   Civil and disaster relief.
411.760   General assistance.
412.115   Aid to blind.
412.610   Aid to disabled.
413.610   Old-age assistance.
414.095   Medical assistance.
418.040   AFDC.
655.530   Injured inmates benefits.
656.234   Workers' compensation.
657.855   Unemployment compensation.

TOOLS OF TRADE
23.160   Tools, implements, apparatus, team, harness, or library, up to $3,000 total (**).

ALIMONY AND CHILD SUPPORT
23.160   Alimony and child support needed to support.

INSURANCE
732.240   Life insurance proceeds if policy prohibits use to pay creditors.
743.046   Life insurance proceeds or cash value if you are not the insured.
743.047   Group life insurance policy or proceeds.
743.049   Annuity contract benefits up to $500 per month.
743.050   Health or disability insurance proceeds, dividends, interest, loan, cash or surrender value.
748.225   Fraternal benefit society benefits.

MISCELLANEOUS
68.420   Business partnership property.
471.301   Liquor licenses.
Other   Add any applicable Federal Non-Bankruptcy Exemptions.

PENNSYLVANIA

Purdon's Pennsylvania Statutes Annotated, Title 42, Section 8123 (42 Pa.C.S.A. §8123). Compare federal exemptions.

HOMESTEAD

None, but tenancies by the entirety are exempt without limit as to debts of one spouse [*In re McCormick*, 18 B.R. 911 (W.D. Pa. 1982)].

PERSONAL PROPERTY

42-8123 $300 of any property.

42-8124 Clothing, bibles, school books, sewing machines, uniform and accoutrements.

42-8125 Tangible personal property at an international exhibition sponsored by the U.S. government.

WAGES

42-8127 Earned but unpaid wages.

PENSIONS

16-4716	County employees.
24-8533	Public school employees.
42-8124	Self-employment benefits; private retirement benefits if clause prohibits use to pay creditors, to extent they are tax deferred, and limited to $15,000 per year deposited, and must be deposited at least 1 year before filing.
53-764;53-776; 53-23666	Police officers.
53-881.115	Municipal employees.
53-13445; 53-23572; 53-39383	City employees.
71-5953	State employees.

PUBLIC BENEFITS

42-8124	Workers' compensation.
43-863	Unemployment compensation.
51-20012	Veterans' benefits.
51-20098	Korean conflict veterans' benefits.
71-180-7.10	Crime victims' compensation.

INSURANCE

42-8124 No-fault automobile insurance proceeds; accident or disability benefits; group life insurance policy or proceeds; fraternal benefit society benefits; life insurance proceeds if policy prohibits use to pay creditors; life insurance annuity contract payments, proceeds or cash value up to $100 per month; life insurance annuity policy, proceeds or cash value if beneficiary is descendent's spouse, child or other dependent.

MISCELLANEOUS

15-8341 Business partnership property.

Other Add any applicable Federal Non-Bankruptcy Exemptions.

RHODE ISLAND

General Laws of Rhode Island, Section 7-8-25 (G.L.R.I. §7-8-25). Ignore "title" and "chapter" numbers; look for "section" numbers. Compare with federal exemptions.

PERSONAL PROPERTY
7-8-25	Consumer cooperative association holdings up to $50.
9-26-3	Body of a deceased person.
9-26-4	Clothing needed; furniture and family stores of a housekeeper, beds and bedding up to $1,000 total; books up to $300; burial plot; debt owed to you which is secured by a promissory note or bill of exchange.

WAGES
9-26-4	Earned but unpaid wages up to $50; wages of spouse; earned but unpaid wages of a seaman, or if you have received welfare during the year prior to filing for bankruptcy; wages paid to the poor by a charitable organization; earnings of a minor child.
30-7-9	Earned but unpaid wages of a military member on active duty.

PENSIONS
9-26-4	ERISA-qualified benefits.
9-26-5	Police officers and firefighters.
28-17-4	Private employees.
36-10-34	State and municipal employees.

PUBLIC BENEFITS
28-33-27	Workers' compensation.
28-41-32	State disability benefits.
28-44-58	Unemployment compensation.
30-7-9	Veterans' disability or survivor benefits.
40-6-14	AFDC; general assistance; aid to blind, aged and disabled.

TOOLS OF TRADE
9-26-4	Working tools up to $500; library of a professional in practice.

INSURANCE
27-4-11	Life insurance proceeds, dividends, interest, loan, cash or surrender value if beneficiary is not the insured.
27-4-12	Life insurance proceeds if policy prohibits use to pay creditors.
27-18-24	Accident or illness proceeds, benefits, dividends, interest, loan, cash or surrender value.
27-25-18	Fraternal benefit society benefits.
28-41-32	Temporary disability insurance.

MISCELLANEOUS
7-12-36	Business partnership property.
Other	Add any applicable Federal Non-Bankruptcy Exemptions.

SOUTH CAROLINA

Code of Laws of South Carolina, Title 15, Section 15-41-30 (C.L.S.C. §15-41-30). Ignore volume numbers; look for "title" numbers.

HOMESTEAD
15-41-30   Real property, including coop, up to $5,000.(**)

PERSONAL PROPERTY
15-41-30   Motor vehicle up to $1,200; clothing, household goods, furnishings, appliances, books, musical instruments, animals and crops up to $2,500 total; jewelry up to $500; health aids; personal injury and wrongful death recoveries.
15-41-30   IN LIEU OF HOMESTEAD: Burial plot up to $5,000.(**)
15-41-30   IN LIEU OF HOMESTEAD AND BURIAL PLOT: Cash and other liquid assets up to $1,000.

PENSIONS
9-1-1680   Public employees.
9-8-190   Judges and solicitors.
9-9-180   General assembly members.
9-11-270   Police officers.
9-13-230   Firefighters.
15-41-30   ERISA-qualified benefits.

PUBLIC BENEFITS
15-41-30   Unemployment compensation; social security; veterans' benefits.
15-41-30; 16-3-1300   Crime victims' compensation.
42-9-360   Workers' compensation.
43-5-190   AFDC; general relief; aid to blind, aged and disabled.

TOOLS OF TRADE
15-41-30   Tools, books and implements of trade up to $750 total.

ALIMONY AND CHILD SUPPORT
15-41-30   Alimony and child support.

INSURANCE
15-41-30   Unmatured life insurance contract (but a credit insurance policy is not exempt); disability or illness benefits; life insurance proceeds from a policy for a person you depended upon which is needed for support; life insurance dividends, interest, loan, cash or surrender value from a policy for a person you depended upon up to $4,000.
38-37-870 Fraternal benefit society benefits.
38-63-40   Life insurance proceeds for a spouse or child up to $25,000.
38-63-50   Life insurance proceeds if policy prohibits use to pay creditors.

MISCELLANEOUS
33-41-720 Business partnership property.
Other   Add any applicable Federal Non-Bankruptcy Exemptions.

SOUTH DAKOTA

South Dakota Codified Laws, Title 43, Chapter 31, Section 43-31-1 (S.D.C.L. §43-31-1). Ignore volume numbers; look for "title" numbers.

HOMESTEAD
43-31-1; 43-31-2   Real property, including mobile home if larger than 240 square feet and registered in the State at least 6 months prior to filing bankruptcy, of unlimited value; but cannot exceed 1 acre in a town or 160 acres elsewhere. Sale proceeds are exempt for 1 year after sale up to $30,000 (of unlimited value if you are an unmarried widow or widower, or are over 70). Spouse or child of a deceased owner may also claim exemption. Can't include gold or silver mine, mill or smelter. 43-31-5.

PERSONAL PROPERTY
43-45-2   All debtors may claim clothing; food and fuel to last 1 year; bible; books up to $200; pictures; church pew; burial plot.

43-45-4   Non-head of family may also claim $2,000 of any personal property.

43-45-5   Head of family may claim either $4,000 of any personal property, OR furniture and bedding up to $200; books and musical instruments up to $200; tools and library of professional up to $300; tools of a mechanic and stock in trade up to $200; farm machinery, utensils, wagon, sleigh, 2 plows, harrow, and tackle for teams up to $1,250 total; 2 yoke of oxen or a span of horses or mules; 2 cows, 5 swine, 25 sheep with lambs under 6 months, wool, yarn or cloth of sheep, and food for all to last 1 year.

WAGES
15-20-12   Earned wages owing 60 days prior to filing for bankruptcy, needed for support.

24-8-10   Wages of prisoners in work programs.

PENSIONS
3-12-115   Public employees.

9-16-47   City employees.

PUBLIC BENEFITS
28-7-16   AFDC.

61-6-28   Unemployment compensation.

62-4-42   Workers' compensation.

TOOLS OF TRADE
   See Personal Property.

INSURANCE
43-45-6   Life insurance proceeds if beneficiary is surviving spouse or child up to $10,000.

58-12-4   Health benefits up to $20,000; endowment or life insurance policy, proceeds or cash value up to $20,000(*).

58-12-8   Annuity contract proceeds up to $250 per month.

58-15-70   Life insurance proceeds if policy prohibits use to pay creditors.

58-37-68   Fraternal benefit society benefits.

MISCELLANEOUS
48-4-14   Business partnership property.

Other   Add any applicable Federal Non-Bankruptcy Exemptions.

TENNESSEE

Tennessee Code Annotated, Title 26, Section 26-2-301 (T.C.A. §26-2-301). Ignore volume numbers; look for "section" numbers.

HOMESTEAD
26-2-301 $5,000; $7,500 for joint owners. Tenancies by the entirety are exempt without limit as to debts of one spouse [*In re Arango*, 136 B.R. 740; affirmed 992 F.2d 611 (6th Cir. 1993)]. Spouse or child of deceased owner may claim. May also claim a life estate or a 2 to 15 year lease.

PERSONAL PROPERTY
26-2-102 $4,000 of any personal property.

26-2-103   Clothing and storage containers; schools books, pictures, portraits, and bible.

26-2-111   Health aids; lost earnings payments for yourself or a person you depended upon; personal injury recoveries, not including pain and suffering, up to $7,500; wrongful death recoveries up to $10,000 (LIMIT: total of personal injury claims, wrongful death claims and crime victims' compensation cannot exceed $15,000).

26-2-305; 46-2-102   Burial plot up to 1 acre.

WAGES
26-2-106;

26-2-107   Minimum of 75% of earned but unpaid wages, plus $2.50 per week per child. Judge may approve more for low income debtor.

PENSIONS
8-36-111   Public employees.

26-2-104   State and local government employees.

26-2-111   ERISA-qualified benefits.

45-9-909   Teachers.

PUBLIC BENEFITS
26-2-111   Unemployment compensation; veterans' benefits; social security; local public assistance.

26-2-111;

29-13-111   Crime victims' compensation up to $5,000, but see" LIMIT" under Personal Property above.

50-6-223   Workers' compensation.

71-2-216   Old-age assistance.

71-3-121   AFDC.

71-4-117   Aid to blind.

71-4-1112   Aid to disabled.

TOOLS OF TRADE
26-2-111   Tools, books and implements of trade up to $750.

ALIMONY AND CHILD SUPPORT
26-2-111   Alimony which is owed for at least 30 days prior to filing for bankruptcy.

INSURANCE
26-2-110   Disability, accident or health benefits, for a resident and citizen of Tennessee.

26-2-111   Disability or illness benefits.

26-2-304   Homeowners' insurance proceeds up to $5,000.

56-7-201   Life insurance proceeds or cash value if beneficiary is the debtor's spouse, child or other dependent.

56-25-208   Fraternal benefit society benefits.

MISCELLANEOUS
61-1-124   Business partnership property.

Other   Add any applicable Federal Non-Bankruptcy Exemptions.

TEXAS

There are two sets of books that contain the Texas laws. One is called *Vernon's* Texas Civil Statutes, and is arranged by section number. The other is called *Vernon's* Texas Codes Annotated, and is divided into subjects, such as "Property," Insurance," "Human Resources," etc. The references given below that begin with just a number are references to the Civil Statutes (such as "42.002"). The references that begin with a word are references to the subject volume or volumes of the Codes (such as "Prop. 41.001"). Compare Federal Bankruptcy Exemptions.

HOMESTEAD
Prop. 41.001; Prop. 41.002 Unlimited amount, but cannot exceed 1 acre in a city, town or village, or 100 acres (200 acres for family) elsewhere. Sale proceeds are exempt for 6 months after sale. You need not occupy at filing, as long as you don't acquire another home.

PERSONAL PROPERTY
Prop. 41.001 Burial plots.
Prop. 42.001 Prescribed health aids.
Prop. 42.002 Home furnishings, including family heirlooms; food; clothing; jewelry up to 25% of the SPECIAL LIMIT stated below; 2 firearms; athletic & sporting equipment (includes bicycles); 1 motor vehicle for each adult with drivers license or who relies on another to operate a vehicle; 2 horses, mules, or donkeys, with saddle, blanket & bridle for each; 12 head cattle; 60 head other livestock; 120 fowl; food on hand for these animals; and household pets. SPECIAL LIMIT: Total of all items under Property 42.002 (including tools of trade and cash value of life insurance) cannot exceed $30,000 total ($60,000 for head of family).

WAGES
Prop. 42.001 Current wages for personal services; and unpaid commissions for personal services up to 25% of the SPECIAL LIMIT stated above.

PENSIONS
110B-21.005	State employees.	6243d-1;6243j; 6243g-1	Police officers.
110B-31.005	Teachers.	6243e;6243e.1; 6243e.2	Firefighters.
110B-41.004	Judges.	6243g; 110B-61.006	Municipal employees.
110B-51.006	County and district employees.	Prop. 42.0021	Church benefits; ERISA-qualified retirement benefits to extent tax-deferred, including IRAs, Keoghs & simplified employee plans.
6228f	Law enforcement officers' survivors.		

PUBLIC BENEFITS
5221b-13	Unemployment compensation.	Hum.Res. 31.040	AFDC.
8306-3	Workers' compensation.	Hum.Res. 32.036	Medical assistance.
8309-1	Crime victims' compensation.		

TOOLS OF TRADE
Prop. 42.002 Tools, books, and equipment, including motor vehicles and boats used in trade or profession; and farming or ranching vehicles and implements.

INSURANCE
Insur. 3.50-2 Texas employee uniform group insurance.
Insur. 3.50-3 Texas state college or university employee benefits.
Insur. 3.50-4 Retired public school employees group insurance.
Insur. 10.28 Fraternal benefit society benefits.
Insur. 21.22 Life, health, accident or annuity benefits; life insurance proceeds if policy prohibits use to pay creditors.
Prop. 42.002 Life insurance cash value if beneficiary is debtor or family member.

MISCELLANEOUS
6132b-25 Business partnership property.
Other Add any applicable Federal Non-Bankruptcy Exemptions.

UTAH

Utah Code Annotated 1953, Title 78, Chapter 23, Section 78-23-3 (U.C.A. §78-23-3). Ignore volume numbers; look for "title" numbers.

HOMESTEAD
78-23-3   Real property, mobile home or water rights up to $8,000, plus $2,000 for spouse and $500 for each other dependent. Homestead declaration must be filed before selling home.

PERSONAL PROPERTY
78-23-5   Clothing, except furs and jewelry; refrigerator, freezer, stove, washer, dryer and sewing machine; health aids needed; food to last 3 months; beds and bedding; carpets; artwork done by, or depicting, a family member; burial plot; personal injury recoveries for yourself or a person you depend upon; wrongful death recoveries for a person you depended upon.

78-23-8   Furnishings and appliances up to $500; books, musical instruments and animals up to $500 total; heirloom or sentimental item up to $500.

78-23-9   Proceeds for damaged personal property.

WAGES
70C-7-103   Minimum of 75% of earned but unpaid wages. Judge may approve more for low income debtor.

PENSIONS
49-1-609   Public employees.

78-23-5   ERISA-qualified benefits.

78-23-6   Any pension needed for support.

PUBLIC BENEFITS
35-1-80   Workers' compensation.

35-2-35   Occupational disease disability benefits.

35-4-18   Unemployment compensation.

55-15-32   AFDC; general assistance.

63-63-21   Crime victims' compensation.

78-23-5   Veterans' benefits.

TOOLS OF TRADE
39-1-47   Military property of a national guard member.

78-23-8   Motor vehicle used in business or trade up to $1,500; tools, books and implements of trade up to $1,500.

ALIMONY AND CHILD SUPPORT
78-23-5   Child support.

78-23-6   Alimony needed for support.

INSURANCE
31A-9-603   Fraternal benefit society benefits.

78-23-5   Disability, illness, medical or hospital benefits.

78-23-6   Life insurance proceeds if beneficiary is insured's spouse or other dependent, needed for support.

78-23-7   Life insurance policy cash surrender value up to $1,500.

MISCELLANEOUS
48-1-22   Business partnership property.

Other   Add any applicable Federal Non-Bankruptcy Exemptions.

VERMONT

Vermont Statutes Annotated, Title 27, Section 101 (27 V.S.A. §101). Look for "title" numbers. Compare Federal Bankruptcy Exemptions.

HOMESTEAD
27-101 $30,000. Tenancies by the entirety are exempt without limit as to debts of one spouse [In re *McQueen*, 21 B.R. 736 (D. Ver. 1982)]. May include outbuildings, rents, issues and profits. Spouse of a deceased owner may claim.

PERSONAL PROPERTY
12-2740   Motor vehicles up to $2,500; clothing, goods, furnishings, appliances, books, musical instruments, animals and crops up to $2,500 total; refrigerator, stove, freezer, water heater, heating unit and sewing machines; health aids; bank deposits up to $700; wedding ring; jewelry up to $500; 500 gallons of oil, 5 tons of coal or 10 cords of firewood; 500 gallons of bottled gas; lost future earnings for yourself or a person you depended upon; personal injury and wrongful death recoveries for a person you depended upon; 1 cow, 10 sheep, 10 chickens, 3 swarms of bees, and feed to last 1 winter; 1 yoke of oxen or steers, 2 horses, 2 harnesses, 2 halters, 2 chains, 1 plow and 1 ox yoke; growing crops up to $5,000.
12-2740 $400 of any property; plus $7,000, less any amount claimed for clothing, goods, furnishings, appliances, books, musical instruments, animals, crops, motor vehicle, jewelry, tools of trade and growing crops, of any property.

WAGES
12-3170   Minimum of 75% of earned but unpaid wages (judge may approve more for low income debtor); all wages if you received welfare during the 2 months prior to filing for bankruptcy.

PENSIONS
3-476   State employees.
12-2740   Self-directed accounts, including IRAs and Keoghs, up to $10,000; other pensions.
16-1946   Teachers.
24-5066   Municipal employees.

PUBLIC BENEFITS
12-2740   Veterans' benefits, social security and crime victims' compensation needed for support.
21-681   Workers' compensation.
21-1376   Unemployment compensation.
33-2575   AFDC; general assistance; aid to blind, aged and disabled.

TOOLS OF TRADE
12-2740   Tools and books of trade up to $5,000.

ALIMONY AND CHILD SUPPORT
12-2740   Alimony and child support needed for support.

INSURANCE
8-3705   Life insurance proceeds if policy prohibits use to pay creditors.
8-3706   Life insurance proceeds if insured is not the beneficiary.
8-3708   Group life or health benefits.
8-3709   Annuity contract benefits up to $350 per month.
8-4086   Health benefits up to $200 per month.
8-4478   Fraternal benefit society benefits.
12-2740   Unmatured life insurance contract (but not credit insurance policy); disability or illness benefits needed for support; life insurance proceeds for a person you depended upon.

MISCELLANEOUS
11-1282   Business partnership property.
Other   Add any applicable Federal Non-Bankruptcy Exemptions.

VIRGINIA

Code of Virginia 1950, Title 34, Section 34-4 (C.V. §34-4). Ignore "chapter" numbers; look for "title" and "section" numbers.

HOMESTEAD (**)
34-4 $5,000 [$7,000 for veterans with a 40% V.A.-rated service connected disability (34-4.1)], plus $500 per dependent. Tenancies by the entirety are exempt without limitation as to debts of one spouse [*In re Harris*, 155 B.R. 948 (E.D.Va. 1993)]. Includes rents and profits (34-18). Sale proceeds are exempt (34-20). Must file homestead declaration prior to filing for bankruptcy (34-6).

PERSONAL PROPERTY
34-4.1 $2,000 of any property of a disabled veteran who is a householder.
34-13   Unused homestead.
34-26   ONLY IF YOU ARE A HOUSEHOLDER YOU MAY CLAIM: Motor vehicle up to $2,000; wearing apparel up to $1,000; household furnishings up to $5,000; family portraits and heirlooms up to $5,000; burial plot; wedding and engagement rings, family Bible; animals owned as pets, provided they are not raised for sale or profit; and medically prescribed health aids.
34-13   IN LIEU OF HOMESTEAD: $5,000 of any personal property.

WAGES
34-29   Minimum of 75% of earned but unpaid wages or pension payments. Judge may approve more for low income debtor.

PENSIONS
51-111.15   State employees.
51-127.7   County employees.
51-180   Judges.

PUBLIC BENEFITS
19.2-368.12   Crime victims' compensation, unless seeking to discharge debt for treatment of crime-related injury.
60.2-600   Unemployment compensation.
63.1-88   AFDC; general relief; aid to blind, aged and disabled.
65.1-82   Workers' compensation.

TOOLS OF TRADE

ANYONE MAY CLAIM:
44-96   Arms, uniforms and equipment of a military member.

IF YOU ARE A HOUSEHOLDER YOU MAY ALSO CLAIM:
34-26   Tools, books, instruments, implements, equipment, and machines, including motor vehicles, vessels, and aircraft, necessary for use in occupation or trade up to $10,000.
34-27   For farmer: tractor, wagon, cart, horses, pair of mules with gear up to $3,000; fertilizer, 2 plows, harvest cradle, 2 iron wedges, pitchfork and rake, up to $1,000.

INSURANCE
38.2-3122   Life insurance proceeds, dividends, interest, loan, cash or surrender value if beneficiary is not the insured.
38.2-3123   If you are a householder, life insurance cash values up to $10,000.
38.2-3339   Group life insurance policy or proceeds.
38.2-3549   Accident, sickness or industrial sick benefits.
38.2-3811   Cooperative life insurance benefits.
38.2-4021   Burial society benefits.
38.2-4118   Fraternal benefit society benefits.
51-111.67:8   Group life or accident insurance for government officials.

MISCELLANEOUS
50-25   Business partnership property.
Other   Add any applicable Federal Non-Bankruptcy Exemptions.

WASHINGTON

West's Revised Code of Washington Annotated, Title 6, Chapter 6.13, Section 6.13.010 (R.C.W.A. §6.13.010). Compare Federal Bankruptcy Exemptions.

HOMESTEAD (*)
6.13.010   Real property or mobile home up to $30,000 [no limit on exemption if you are seeking to discharge a debt based on another state's claim of failure to pay that state income tax on pension or retirement benefits you received while a resident of Washington (6.13.030)]. If property is unimproved or unoccupied at time of filing bankruptcy, you must file a homestead declaration.

PERSONAL PROPERTY
6.15.010   2 motor vehicles up to $2,500 total; clothing, but furs, jewelry & ornaments limited to $1,000 total; household goods, furniture, appliances, food, fuel, home and yard equipment up to $2,700 total; books up to $1,000; pictures and keepsakes; private libraries up to $1,500; $1,000 of any other personal property, but not more than $100 of it in cash, bank deposits, stocks, bonds or other securities.
68.20.120   Burial plots if sold by a non-profit cemetery association.

WAGES
6.27.150   Minimum of 75% of earned but unpaid wages. Judge may approve more for low income debtor.

PENSIONS
6.15.020   Federal employees; ERISA-qualified benefits, including IRAs.
41.24.240   Volunteer firefighters.
41.28.200   City employees.
41.40.380   Public employees.
43.43.310   State patrol officers.

PUBLIC BENEFITS
7.68.070;
51.32.040   Crime victims' compensation.
50.40.020   Unemployment compensation.
51.32.040   Industrial insurance (workers' compensation).
74.04.280   General assistance.
74.08.210   Old-age assistance.
74.13.070   AFDC.

TOOLS OF TRADE
6.15.010   Tools and materials used in another person's trade up to $5,000; library, office furniture, equipment and supplies of a physician, surgeon, attorney, clergyman or other professional up to $5,000; farm trucks, tools, equipment, supplies, stock and seed of a farmer up to $5,000.

INSURANCE
6.15.030   Insurance proceeds for destroyed exempt property.
46.18.400   Disability benefits, proceeds, dividends, interest, loan, cash or surrender value.
46.18.410   Life insurance proceeds, dividends, interest, loan, cash or surrender value if the insured is not the beneficiary.
46.18.420   Group life insurance policy or proceeds.
46.18.430   Annuity contract proceeds up to $250 per month.
48.36A.180   Fraternal benefit society benefits.

MISCELLANEOUS
25.04.250   Business partnership property.
Other   Add any applicable Federal Non-Bankruptcy Exemptions.

WEST VIRGINIA

West Virginia Code, Chapter 38, Article 10, Section 38-10-4 (.W.V.C. §38-10-4). Ignore volume numbers; look for "chapter" numbers.

HOMESTEAD
38-10-4   Real or personal property used as a residence up to $15,000. Unused portion may be applied to any other property.

PERSONAL PROPERTY
38-10-4   Motor vehicle up to $2,400; clothing, household goods, furnishings, appliances, books, musical instruments, animals and crops up to $400 per item, and $8,000 total; jewelry up to $1,000; health aids; lost earnings payments needed for support; personal injury recoveries, not including pain and suffering, up to $7,500; wrongful death recoveries for a person you depended upon needed for support; $800 of any property.

38-10-4 $7,900, less amount of homestead claimed, of any property.

38-10-4   Burial plot up to $15,000, in lieu of homestead.

WAGES
38-5A-3   80% of earned but unpaid wages. Judge may approve more for low income debtor.

PENSIONS
5-10-46   Public employees.

18-7A-30   Teachers.

38-10-4   ERISA-qualified benefits needed for support.

PUBLIC BENEFITS
9-5-1   AFDC; general assistance; aid to blind, aged and disabled.

14-2A-24; 38-10-4   Crime victims' compensation.

23-4-18   Workers' compensation.

38-10-4   Unemployment compensation; veterans' benefits; social security.

TOOLS OF TRADE
38-4-10   Tools, books and implements of trade up to $1,500.

ALIMONY AND CHILD SUPPORT
38-10-4   Alimony and child support needed for support.

INSURANCE
33-6-27   Life insurance proceeds unless you are policy owner and beneficiary.

33-6-28   Group life insurance policy and proceeds.

33-23-21   Fraternal benefit society benefits.

38-10-4   Unmatured life insurance contract (except for credit life insurance contract); health or disability benefits; life insurance dividends, interest, loan, cash or surrender value for person you depended upon up to $4,000.

48-3-23   Life insurance proceeds or cash value if the beneficiary is a married woman.

MISCELLANEOUS
47-8A-25   Business partnership property.

Other   Add any applicable Federal Non-Bankruptcy Exemptions.

WISCONSIN

West's Wisconsin Statutes Annotated, Section 815.20 (W.S.A. §815.20). Look for "section" numbers. Compare Federal Bankruptcy Exemptions.

HOMESTEAD
815.20 $40,000. Sale proceed exempt for 2 years after sale provided you intend to acquire another home. Must occupy or intend to occupy at time of filing for bankruptcy.

PERSONAL PROPERTY
815.18   Automobile up to $1,200; household goods and furnishings; wearing apparel, keepsakes, jewelry and other articles of adornment, appliances, books, musical instruments, firearms, sporting goods, animals or other items for family use up to $5,000 total; burial plot, monument, tombstone, etc.; and bank deposits up to $1,000; wrongful death proceeds and lost earnings compensation for debtor or person on whom debtor was dependent, to extent necessary to support debtor or family; and personal injury payments for debtor or person upon whom debtor depended, up to $25,000.

WAGES
815.18   75% of net wages, but limited to amount necessary for support, and no less that 30 times the state or federal minimum wage, whichever is greater.

PENSIONS
40.08   Public employees.
66.81   Certain municipal employees in a city of more 150,000 or more in population.
815.18   Police officers, firefighters, military pensions, and public and private retirement benefits (including plans for self-employed persons).

PUBLIC BENEFITS
45.35	Veterans' benefits.	108.13	Unemployment compensation.
49.41	AFDC; other social service payments.	949.07	Crime victims' compensation.
102.27	Workers' compensation.		

TOOLS OF TRADE
815.18   Equipment, inventory, farm products, and professional books used in the business of the debtor or a dependent, up to $7,500.

ALIMONY AND CHILD SUPPORT
815.18   Alimony & child support needed for support.

INSURANCE
614.96   Fraternal benefit society benefits.
632.42   Life insurance proceeds if policy prohibits use to pay creditors.
815.18   Unmatured life insurance contracts, and up to $4,000 in value in accrued dividends, interest or loan value (except for credit life contracts) if owned by debtor and insuring debtor, dependent, or person debtor is dependent upon; federal disability benefits; life insurance proceeds if debtor was dependent upon insured, to extent necessary to support debtor or family; and fire insurance proceeds received during prior 2 years for destroyed exempt property.

MISCELLANEOUS
178.21   Business partnership property.
Other   Add any applicable Federal Non-Bankruptcy Exemptions.

WYOMING

Wyoming Statutes Annotated, Title 1, Chapter 20, Section 1-20-101 (W.S.A. §1-20-101). Ignore volume numbers; look for "title" numbers.

HOMESTEAD (**)
1-20-101; 1-20-104   Real property up to $10,000; house trailer up to $6,000. Tenancies by the entirety are exempt without limit as to debts of one spouse [*In re Anselmi*, 52 B.R. 479 (D. Wyo. 1985)]. Spouse or child of deceased owner may claim; Must occupy at time of filing for bankruptcy.

PERSONAL PROPERTY
1-20-105   Clothing and wedding rings up to $1,000 total.
1-20-106   Household articles, furniture, bedding and food up to $2,000 per person in the home; school books, pictures and bible; motor vehicle up to $2,000.
1-20-106;
35-8-104   Burial plot.
26-32-102   Pre-paid funeral contracts.

WAGES
1-15-511   Minimum of 75% of earned but unpaid wages. Judge may approved more for low income debtor.
17-16-308   Wages of inmates on work release.
19-2-501   Earnings of national guard members.

PENSIONS
1-20-110   Private or public retirement funds or accounts.
9-3-426   Public employees.
9-3-620   Highway officers, criminal investigators, and game and fish wardens.
15-5-209   Payments being received by police officers and firefighters.

PUBLIC BENEFITS
1-40-113   Crime victims' compensation.
27-3-319   Unemployment compensation.
27-14-702   Workers' compensation.
42-2-113   AFDC; general assistance.

TOOLS OF TRADE
1-20-106   Motor vehicle, tools, implements, team and stock in trade to $2,000; library and implements of a professional up to $2,000.

INSURANCE
26-15-129   Life insurance proceeds if insured is not the beneficiary.
26-15-130   Disability benefits if policy prohibits use to pay creditors.
26-15-131   Group life or disability policy or proceeds.
26-15-132   Annuity contract proceeds up to $350 per month.
26-15-133   Life insurance proceeds if policy prohibits use to pay creditors.
26-29-116   Fraternal benefit society benefits.

MISCELLANEOUS
12-4-604   Liquor licenses and malt beverage permits.
17-13-502   Business partnership property.
Other   Add any applicable Federal Non-Bankruptcy Exemptions.

APPENDIX B
FORMS

This appendix contains the forms referred to in the various sections of this book. To use them, you should first make photocopies of the ones you will need.

An asterisk (*) following the title of a form indicates that the form also has a continuation sheet to be used for additional information. The continuation sheet will be found immediately after the form in this appendix.

In 1991, bankruptcy forms were standardized throughout the country. However, you may find that your particular bankruptcy court has certain other required forms. Before you begin to prepare your forms, you should call the court clerk's office and ask if there are any special required forms. The current bankruptcy rules require the courts to accept the forms used in this book.

TABLE OF FORMS

Form 1: Income and Expense Worksheet 153

Form 2: Property Worksheet 154

Form 3: Debt Worksheet 155

Form 4: Voluntary Petition 156

Form 5: Application to Pay Filing Fee in Installments 158

Form 6: Summary of Schedules. 159

FORM 7: SCHEDULE A - REAL PROPERTY 160

FORM 8: SCHEDULE B - PERSONAL PROPERTY* 161

FORM 9: SCHEDULE C - PROPERTY CLAIMED AS EXEMPT 164

FORM 10: SCHEDULE D - CREDITORS HOLDING SECURED CLAIMS* 165

FORM 11: SCHEDULE E - CREDITORS HOLDING UNSECURED PRIORITY CLAIMS* 167

FORM 12: SCHEDULE F - CREDITORS HOLDING UNSECURED NONPRIORITY CLAIMS* 169

FORM 13: SCHEDULE G - EXECUTORY CONTRACTS AND UNEXPIRED LEASES 171

FORM 14: SCHEDULE H - CODEBTORS 172

FORM 15: SCHEDULE I - CURRENT INCOME OF INDIVIDUAL DEBTOR(S) 173

FORM 16: SCHEDULE J - CURRENT EXPENDITURES OF INDIVIDUAL DEBTOR(S) 174

FORM 17: DECLARATION CONCERNING DEBTOR'S SCHEDULES 175

FORM 18: STATEMENT OF FINANCIAL AFFAIRS 176

FORM 19: CHAPTER 7 INDIVIDUAL DEBTOR'S STATEMENT OF INTENTION 186

FORM 20: CHAPTER 13 PLAN 187

FORM 21: MAILING MATRIX 189

FORM 22: LETTER NOTIFYING CREDITORS 190

FORM 23: SUGGESTION OF BANKRUPTCY 191

FORM 24: CERTIFICATE OF MAILING 192

FORM 25: LETTER TO CREDITORS 193

FORM 26: MONTHLY BUDGET 194

FORM 27: AMENDMENT COVER SHEET 195

FORM 28: MOTION TO CONVERT TO CHAPTER 7 196

INCOME AND EXPENSE WORKSHEET

INCOME (Monthly):
    Take Home Pay (wages, salary, commissions)   _____
    Self Employment Income   _____
    Interest and Dividends   _____
    Income From Real Estate   _____
    Retirement Income   _____
    Alimony or Support Payments   _____
    Other:_____   _____
    _____   _____

TOTAL MONTHLY INCOME   _____

EXPENSES (Monthly):
    Mortgage or Rent   _____
    Homeowners/Renters Insurance   _____
    Real Estate Taxes   _____
    Electricity   _____
    Gas   _____
    Water   _____
    Telephone   _____
    Garbage Pick-up   _____
    Other:_____   _____
    Home Repair/Maintenance   _____
    Auto Loan   _____
    Other Installment Loan Payments:

    _____   _____
    _____   _____
    _____   _____
    _____   _____

    Auto Insurance   _____
    Gasoline   _____
    Auto Repairs/Maintenance   _____
    Food   _____
    Clothing   _____
    Medical, Dental, and Medicines   _____
    Life Insurance   _____
    Laundry   _____
    Recreation/Travel/Entertainment   _____
    Education   _____
    License Fees, Dues, Memberships   _____
    Other Taxes   _____
    Other:_____   _____

    _____   _____
    _____   _____
    _____   _____
    _____   _____

TOTAL MONTHLY EXPENSES   _____

DEFICIT (Total Income - Total Expenses)   _____

PROPERTY WORKSHEET

(1) PROPERTY	(2) VALUE	(3) AMT. OWED	(4) EQUITY	(5) EXEMPT	(6) SECURED
Real Estate:					
Autos, etc.:					
Boats, etc.:					
Cash on hand:					
Bank accts:					
Clothing:					
Jewelry:					
Household Goods:					
Collections:					
Sports Equip:					
Trade tools:					
Investments:					
Insurance:					
Other prop:					
TOTALS:					

DEBT WORKSHEET

form 3

	(1) LENDER	(2) ITEM	(3) BALANCE	(4) SECURED	(5) DISCHARGEABLE
Real Estate:					
Autos, etc.:					
Boats, etc.:					
Credit Cards:					
Student Loans:					
Taxes Owed:					
Other Debts:					
TOTALS:					

United States Bankruptcy Court
_____District of _____

VOLUNTARY PETITION

IN RE (Name of debtor-if individual, enter Last, First, Middle)	NAME OF JOINT DEBTOR (Spouse) (Last, First, Middle)
ALL OTHER NAMES used by the debtor in the last 6 years (include married, maiden, and trade names)	ALL OTHER NAMES used by the joint debtor in the last 6 years (include married, maiden, and trade names)
SOC. SEC./TAX I.D. NO. (if more than one, state all)	SOC. SEC./TAX I.D. NO. (if more than one, state all)
STREET ADDRESS OF DEBTOR (No. and street, city, state, and zip code)	STREET ADDRESS OF JOINT DEBTOR (No. and street, city, state, and zip code)
COUNTY OF RESIDENCE OR PRINCIPAL PLACE OF BUSINESS	COUNTY OF RESIDENCE OR PRINCIPAL PLACE OF BUSINESS
MAILING ADDRESS OF DEBTOR (if different from street address)	MAILING ADDRESS OF JOINT DEBTOR (if different from street address)

LOCATION OF PRINCIPAL ASSETS OF BUSINESS DEBTOR (if different from addresses listed above)

VENUE (Check one box)

☐ Debtor has been domiciled or has had a residence, principal place of business, or principal assets in this District for 180 days immediately preceding the date of the petition or for a longer part of such 180 days than in any other District.

☐ There is a bankruptcy case concerning debtor's affiliate, general partner, or partnership pending in this District.

INFORMATION REGARDING DEBTOR (Check applicable boxes)

TYPE OF DEBTOR
☐ Individual   ☐ Corporation Publicly Held
☐ Joint (Husband & Wife)   ☐ Corporation Not Publicly Held
☐ Partnership   ☐ Municipality
☐ Other _____

NATURE OF DEBT
☐ Non-Business/Consumer   ☐ Business - Complete A & B below

A. TYPE OF BUSINESS (Check one box)

☐ Farming   ☐ Transportation   ☐ Commodity Broker
☐ Professional   ☐ Manufacturing/   ☐ Construction
☐ Retail/Wholesale   Mining   ☐ Real Estate
☐ Railroad   ☐ Stockbroker   ☐ Other Business

B. BRIEFLY DESCRIBE NATURE OF BUSINESS

CHAPTER OR SECTION OF BANKRUPTCY CODE UNDER WHICH THE PETITION IS FILED (Check one box)

☐ Chapter 7   ☐ Chapter 11   ☐ Chapter 13
☐ Chapter 9   ☐ Chapter 12   ☐ Sec 304-Case Ancillary to Foreign Proceeding

FILING FEE (Check one box)
☐ Filing fee attached
☐ Filing fee to be paid in installments (Applicable to individuals only) Must attach signed application for the court's consideration certifying that the debtor is unable to pay fee except in installments. Rule 1006(b).

NAME AND ADDRESS OF LAW FIRM OR ATTORNEY

Telephone No.

NAME(S) OF ATTORNEY(S) DESIGNATED TO REPRESENT THE DEBTOR (Print or Type Names)

☐ Debtor is not represented by an attorney.

STATISTICAL ADMINISTRATIVE INFORMATION (28 U.S.C. §604)
(Estimates only) (Check applicable boxes)

THIS SPACE FOR COURT USE ONLY

☐ Debtor estimates that funds will be available for distribution to unsecured creditors.
☐ Debtor estimates that, after any exempt property is excluded and administrative expenses paid, there will be no funds available for distribution to unsecured creditors.

ESTIMATED NUMBER OF CREDITORS

1-15	16-49	50-99	100-199	200-999	1000-over
☐	☐	☐	☐	☐	☐

ESTIMATED ASSETS (In thousands of dollars)

Under 90	90-99	100-499	500-999	1000-9999	10,000-99,000	100,000-over
☐	☐	☐	☐	☐	☐	☐

ESTIMATED LIABILITIES (In thousands of dollars)

Under 90	90-99	100-499	500-999	1000-9999	10,000-99,000	100,000-over
☐	☐	☐	☐	☐	☐	☐

EST. NO. OF EMPLOYEES - CH. 11 & 12 ONLY

0	1-19	20-99	100-999	1000-over
☐	☐	☐	☐	☐

EST. NO. OF EQUITY SECURITY HOLDERS - CH. 11 & 12 ONLY

0	1-19	20-99	100-999	1000-over
☐	☐	☐	☐	☐

FILING OF PLAN

For Chapter 9, 11, 12 and 13 cases only. Check appropriate box.

☐ A copy of debtor's proposed plan dated_____ is attached.

☐ Debtor intends to file a plan within the time allowed by statute, rule, or order of the court.

PRIOR BANKRUPTCY CASE FILED WITHIN LAST 6 YEARS (if more than one, attach additional sheet)

Location Where Filed	Case Number	Date Filed

PENDING BANKRUPTCY CASE FILED BY ANY SPOUSE, PARTNER, OR AFFILIATE OF THE DEBTOR (if more than one, attach additional sheet)

Name of Debtor	Case Number	Date
Relationship	District	Judge

REQUEST FOR RELIEF

Debtor requests relief in accordance with the chapter of title 11, United States Code, specified in this petition.

SIGNATURES

ATTORNEY

X_____

Attorney I.D. Number_____

_____
Date

INDIVIDUAL/JOINT DEBTOR(S)	CORPORATE OR PARTNERSHIP DEBTOR
I declare under penalty of perjury that the information provided in this petition is true and correct.	I declare under penalty of perjury that the information provided in this petition is true and correct, and that the filing of this petition on behalf of the debtor has been authorized.
X_____ Signature of Debtor	X_____ Signature of Authorized Individual
_____ Date	_____ Print or Type Name of Authorized Individual
X_____ Signature of Joint Debtor	_____ Title of Individual Authorized by Debtor to File this Petition
_____ Date	_____ Date

EXHIBIT "A" (To be completed if debtor is a corporation requesting relief under chapter 11.)
☐ Exhibit "A" is attached and made a part of this petition.

TO BE COMPLETED BY INDIVIDUAL CHAPTER 7 DEBTOR WITH PRIMARILY CONSUMER DEBTS (See P.L. 90-353, Sec. 322)

I am aware that I may proceed under chapter 7, 11, or 12, or 13 of title 11, United States Code, understand the relief available under each such chapter, and choose to proceed under chapter 7 of such title.

X_____   _____
Signature of Debtor   Date

X_____   _____
Signature of Joint Debtor   Date

EXHIBIT "B" (To be completed by attorney for individual chapter 7 debtor(s) with primarily consumer debts.)
I, the attorney for the debtor(s) named in the foregoing petition, declare that I have informed the debtor(s) that (he, she, or they) may proceed under chapter 7, 11, 12, or 13 of title 11, United States Code, and have explained the relief available under each such chapter.

X_____   _____
Signature of Attorney   Date

In re_____   Case No._____

               Debtor   (if known)

APPLICATION TO PAY FILING FEE IN INSTALLMENTS

In accordance with Fed. R. Bankr. P. 1006, application is made for permission to pay the filing fee on the following terms:

$_____with the filing of the petition, and the balance of

$_____ in _____installments, as follows:

          $_____ on or before _____

          $_____ on or before _____

          $_____ on or before _____

          $_____ on or before _____

I certify that I am unable to pay the filing fee except in installments. I further certify that I have not paid any money or transferred any property to an attorney or any other person for services in connection with this case or in connection with any other pending bankruptcy case and that I will not make any payment or transfer any property for services in connection with the case until the filing fee is paid in full.

Date:_____

                                     _____
                                     Applicant

                                     _____
                                     Address of Applicant

                                     _____

ORDER

IT IS ORDERED that the debtor pay the filing fee in installments on the terms set forth in the foregoing application.

IT IS FURTHER ORDERED that until the filing fee is paid in full the debtor shall not pay, and no person shall accept, any money for services in connection with this case, and the debtor shall not relinquish, and no person shall accept, any property as payment for services in connection with this case.

                                    BY THE COURT

Date:_____

                                     _____

UNITED STATES BANKRUPTCY COURT

_____District of _____

In re_____   Case No._____

Debtor   (if known)

SUMMARY OF SCHEDULES

Indicate as to each schedule whether that schedule is attached and state the number of pages in each. Report the totals from Schedules A, B, D, E, F, I, and J in the boxes provided. Add the amounts from Schedules A and B to determine the total amount of the debtor's assets. Add the amounts from Schedules D, E, and F to determine the total amount of the debtor's liabilities.

NAME OF SCHEDULE	ATTACHED (YES/NO)	NO. OF SHEETS	AMOUNTS SCHEDULED		
			ASSETS	LIABILITIES	OTHER
A Real Property			$		
B Personal Property			$		
C Property Claimed as Exempt					
D Creditors Holding Secured Claims				$	
E Creditors Holding Unsecured Priority Claims				$	
F Creditors Holding Unsecured Nonpriority Claims				$	
G Executory Contracts and Unexpired Leases					
H Codebtors					
I Current Income of Individual Debtor(s)					$
J Current Expenditures of Individual Debtor(s)					$

Total Number of Sheets of ALL Schedules:

Total Assets $

Total Liabilities $

159

In re_____   Case No._____
                      Debtor   (if known)

SCHEDULE A - REAL PROPERTY

Except as directed below, list all real property in which the debtor has any legal, equitable, or future interest, including all property owned as a co-tenant, community property, or in which the debtor has a life estate. Include any property in which the debtor holds rights and powers exercisable for the debtor's own benefit. If the debtor is married, state whether the husband, wife, or both own the property by placing an "H", "W", "J", or "C" in the column labeled "Husband, Wife, Joint, or Community." If the debtor holds no interest in real property, write "None" under "Description and Location of Property."

Do not include interests in executory contracts and unexpired leases on this schedule. List them in Schedule G-Executory Contracts and Unexpired Leases.

If an entity claims to have a lien or hold a secured interest in any property, state the amount of the secured claim. See Schedule D. If no entity claims to hold a secured interest in the property, write "None" in the column labeled "Amount of Secured Claim."

If the debtor is an individual or if a joint petition is filed, state the amount of any exemption claimed in the property only in Schedule C-Property Claimed as Exempt.

DESCRIPTION AND LOCATION OF PROPERTY	NATURE OF DEBTOR'S INTEREST IN PROPERTY	HUSBAND, WIFE, JOINT, OR COMMUNITY	CURRENT MARKET VALUE OF DEBTOR'S INTEREST IN PROPERTY, WITHOUT DEDUCTING ANY SECURED CLAIM OR EXEMPTION	AMOUNT OF SECURED CLAIM
		Total	$	

(Report also on Summary of Schedules.)

In re_____   Case No._____

Debtor   (if known)

SCHEDULE B - PERSONAL PROPERTY

Except as directed below, list all personal property of the debtor of whatever kind. If the debtor has no property in one or more of the categories, place an "x" in the appropriate position in the column labeled "None." If additional space is needed in any category, attach a separate sheet properly identified with the case number, and the number of the category. If the debtor is married, state whether husband, wife, or both own the property by placing an "H", "W", "J", or "C" in the column labeled "Husband, Wife, Joint, or Community." If the debtor is an individual or a joint petition is filed, state the amount of any exemption claimed only in Schedule C-Property Claimed as Exempt.

Do not list interests in executory contracts and unexpired leases on this schedule. List them in Schedule G-Executory Contracts and Unexpired Leases.

If the property is being held for the debtor by someone else, state that person's name and address under "Description and Location of Property."

TYPE OF PROPERTY	N O N E	DESCRIPTION AND LOCATION OF PROPERTY	HUSBAND, WIFE, JOINT, OR COMMUNITY	CURRENT MARKET VALUE OF DEBTOR'S INTEREST IN PROPERTY, WITHOUT DEDUCTING ANY SECURED CLAIM OR EXEMPTION
1. Cash on hand.				
2. Checking, savings or other financial accounts, certificates of deposit, or shares in banks, savings and loan, thrift, building and loan, and homestead associations, or credit unions, brokerage houses, or cooperatives.				
3. Security deposits with public utilities, telephone companies landlords, and others.				
4. Household goods and furnishings, including audio, video, and computer equipment.				
5. Books, pictures and other art objects, antiques; stamp, coin, record, tape, compact disc, and other collections or collectibles.				
6. Wearing apparel.				
7. Furs and jewelry.				
8. Firearms and sports, photographic, and other hobby equipment.				
9. Interests in insurance policies. Name insurance company of each policy and itemize surrender or refund value of each.				
10. Annuities. Itemize and name each insurer.				

In re_____   Case No._____
　　　　　　　　Debtor　　　　　　　　　　　　　　　　　(if known)

SCHEDULE B - PERSONAL PROPERTY
(Continuation Sheet)

TYPE OF PROPERTY	N O N E	DESCRIPTION AND LOCATION OF PROPERTY	HUSBAND, WIFE, JOINT, OR COMMUNITY	CURRENT MARKET VALUE OF DEBTOR'S INTEREST IN PROPERTY, WITH-OUT DEDUCTING ANY SECURED CLAIM OR EXEMPTION
11. Interests in IRA, ERISA, Keogh, or other pension or profit sharing plans. Itemize.				
12. Stock and interests in incorporated and unincorporated businesses. Itemize.				
13. Interests in partnerships or joint ventures. Itemize.				
14. Government and corporate bonds and other negotiable and non-negotiable instruments.				
15. Accounts receivable.				
16. Alimony, maintenance, support, and property settlements to which the debtor is or may be entitled. Give particulars.				
17. Other liquidated debts owing debtor including tax refunds. Give particulars.				
18. Equitable or future interests, life estates, and rights or powers exercisable for the benefit of the debtor other than those listed in Schedule of Real Property.				
19. Contingent and noncontingent interests in estate of a decedent, death benefit plan, life insurance policy, or trust.				
20. Other contingent and unliquidated claims of every nature, including tax refunds, counterclaims of the debtor, and rights to setoff claims. Give estimated value of each.				
21. Patents, copyrights, and other intellectual property. Give particulars.				

162

In re_____   Case No._____
        Debtor   (if known)

SCHEDULE B - PERSONAL PROPERTY
(Continuation Sheet)

TYPE OF PROPERTY	N O N E	DESCRIPTION AND LOCATION OF PROPERTY	HUSBAND, WIFE, JOINT, OR COMMUNITY	CURRENT MARKET VALUE OF DEBTOR'S INTEREST IN PROPERTY, WITH-OUT DEDUCTING ANY SECURED CLAIM OR EXEMPTION
22. Licenses, franchises, and other general intangibles. Give particulars.				
23. Automobiles, trucks, trailers, and other vehicles and accessories.				
24. Boats, motors, and accessories.				
25. Aircraft and accessories.				
26. Office equipment, furnishings, and supplies.				
27. Machinery, fixtures, equipment, and supplies used in business.				
28. Inventory.				
29. Animals.				
30. Crops-growing or harvested. Give particulars.				
31. Farming equipment and implements.				
32. Farm supplies, chemicals, and feed.				
33. Other personal property of any kind not already listed. Itemize.				
		_____continuation sheets attached	Total	$

(Include amounts from any continuation sheets attached. Report total also on Summary of Schedules.)

In re_____   Case No._____
                        Debtor   (if known)

SCHEDULE C - PROPERTY CLAIMED AS EXEMPT

Debtor elects the exemptions to which debtor is entitled under:
(Check one box)

☐ 11 U.S.C. § 522(b)(1):   Exemptions provided in 11 U.S.C. §522(d). Note: These exemptions are available only in certain states.

☐ 11 U.S.C. § 522(b)(2):   Exemptions available under applicable nonbankruptcy federal laws, state or local law where the debtor's domicile has been located for the 180 days immediately preceding the filing of the petition, or for a longer portion of the 180-day period than in any other place, and the debtor's interest as a tenant by the entirety or joint tenant to the extent the interest is exempt from process under applicable nonbankruptcy law.

DESCRIPTION OF PROPERTY	SPECIFY LAW PROVIDING EACH EXEMPTION	VALUE OF CLAIMED EXEMPTION	CURRENT MARKET VALUE OF PROPERTY WITHOUT DEDUCTING EXEMPTION

In re_____ Case No._____
　　　　　　Debtor　　　　　　　　　　　　　　(if known)

SCHEDULE D - CREDITORS HOLDING SECURED CLAIMS

State the name, mailing address, including zip code, and account number, if any, of all entities holding claims secured by property of the debtor as of the date of filing of the petition. List creditors holding all types of secured interests such as judgment liens, garnishments, statutory liens, mortgages, deeds of trust, and other security interests. List creditors is alphabetical order to the extent practicable. If all secured creditors will not fit on this page, use the continuations sheet provided.

If any entity other than a spouse in a joint case may be jointly liable on a claim, place an "X" in the column labeled "Codebtor," include the entity on the appropriate schedule of creditors, and complete Schedule H-Codebtors. If a joint petition is filed, state whether husband, wife, both of them, or the marital community may be liable on each claim by placing an "H", "W", "J", or "C" in the column labeled "Husband, Wife, Joint, or Community."

If the claim is contingent, place and "X" in the column labeled "Contingent." If the claim is unliquidated, place an "X" in the column labeled "Unliquidated." If the claim is disputed, place an "X" in the column labeled "Disputed." (You may need to place an "X" in more than one of these three columns.)

Report the total of all claims listed on this schedule in the box labeled "Total" on the last sheet of the completed schedule. Report this total also on the Summary of Schedules.

[ ] Check this box if debtor has no creditors holding secured claims to report on this Schedule D.

CREDITOR'S NAME AND MAILING ADDRESS INCLUDING ZIP CODE	CODEBTOR	HUSBAND, WIFE, JOINT, OR COMMUNITY	DATE CLAIM WAS INCURRED, NATURE OF LIEN, AND DESCRIPTION AND MARKET VALUE OF PROPERTY SUBJECT TO LIEN	CONTINGENT	UNLIQUIDATED	DISPUTED	AMOUNT OF CLAIM WITHOUT DEDUCTING VALUE OF COLLATERAL	UNSECURED PORTION, IF ANY
ACCOUNT NO.								
			VALUE $					
ACCOUNT NO.								
			VALUE $					
ACCOUNT NO.								
			VALUE $					
ACCOUNT NO.								
			VALUE $					
			Subtotal (Total of this page)					
			Total (Use only on last page)					

_____continuation sheets attached

(Report total also on Summary of Schedules)

165

In re_____ Case No._____
         Debtor   (if known)

SCHEDULE D - CREDITORS HOLDING SECURED CLAIMS
(Continuation Sheet)

CREDITOR'S NAME AND MAILING ADDRESS INCLUDING ZIP CODE	CODEBTOR	HUSBAND, WIFE, JOINT, OR COMMUNITY	DATE CLAIM WAS INCURRED, NATURE OF LIEN, AND DESCRIPTION AND MARKET VALUE OF PROPERTY SUBJECT TO LIEN	CONTINGENT	UNLIQUIDATED	DISPUTED	AMOUNT OF CLAIM WITHOUT DEDUCTING VALUE OF COLLATERAL	UNSECURED PORTION, IF ANY
ACCOUNT NO.								
			VALUE $					
ACCOUNT NO.								
			VALUE $					
ACCOUNT NO.								
			VALUE $					
ACCOUNT NO.								
			VALUE $					
ACCOUNT NO.								
			VALUE $					
ACCOUNT NO.								
			VALUE $					
			Subtotal (Total of this page)					
			Total (Use only on last page)					

Sheet no. _____ of _____ continuation sheets attached to Schedule of Creditors Holding Secured Claims

(Report total also on Summary of Schedules)

166

In re_____   Case No._____
             Debtor   (if known)

SCHEDULE E - CREDITORS HOLDING UNSECURED PRIORITY CLAIMS

A complete list of claims entitled to priority, listed separately by type of priority, is to be set forth on the sheets provided. Only holders of unsecured claims entitled to priority should be listed in this schedule. In the boxes provided on the attached sheets, state the name and mailing address, including zip code, and account number, if any, of all entities holding priority claims against the debtor or the property of the debtor, as of the date of the filing of the petition.

If any entity other than a spouse in a joint case may be jointly liable on a claim, place an "X" in the column labeled "Codebtor," include the entity on the appropriate schedule of creditors, and complete Schedule H-Codebtors. If a joint petition is filed, state whether husband, wife, both of them, of the marital community may be liable on each claim by placing an "H", "W", "J", or "C" in the column labeled "Husband, Wife, Joint, or Community."

If the claim is contingent, place an "X" in the column labeled "Contingent." If the claim is unliquidated, place an "X" is the column labeled "Unliquidated." If the claim is disputed, place an "X" in the column labeled "Disputed." (You may need to place an "X" in more than one of these three columns.)

Report the total of claims listed on each sheet in the box labeled "Subtotal" on each sheet. Report the total of all claims listed on this Schedule E in the box labeled "Total" on the last sheet of the completed schedule. Repeat this total also on the Summary of Schedules.

☐ Check this box if the debtor has no creditors holding unsecured priority claims to report on this Schedule E.

TYPES OF PRIORITY CLAIMS (Check the appropriate box(es) below if claims in that category are listed on the attached sheets)

☐ Extensions of credit in an involuntary case

    Claims arising in the ordinary course of the debtor's business or financial affairs after the commencement of the case but before the earlier of the appointment of a trustee or the order for relief. 11 U.S.C. Sec. 507(a)(2).

☐ Wages, salaries, and commissions

    Wages, salaries, and commissions, including vacation, severance, and sick leave pay owing to employees, up to a maximum of $2000 per employee, earned within 90 days immediately preceding the filing of the original petition, or the cessation of business, whichever occurred first, to the extent provided in 11 U.S.C. Sec. 507(a)(3).

☐ Contributions to employee benefit plans

    Money owed to employee benefit plans for services rendered within 180 days immediately preceding the filing of the original petition, or the cessation of business, whichever occurred first, to the extent provided in 11 U.S.C. Sec. 507(a)(4).

☐ Certain farmers and fisherman

    Claims of certain farmers and fisherman, up to a maximum of $2000 per farmer or fisherman, against the debtor, as provided in 11 U.S.C. Sec. 507(a)(5).

☐ Deposits by individuals

    Claims of individuals up to a maximum of $900 for deposits for the purchase, lease, or rental of property or services for personal, family, or household use, that were not delivered or provided. 11 U.S.C. Sec. 507(a)(6).

☐ Taxes and Certain Other Debts Owed to Governmental Units

    Taxes, customs duties, and penalties owing to federal, state, and local governmental units as set forth in 11 U.S.C. Sec. 507(a)(7).

_____continuation sheets attached

In re_____ Case No._____
  Debtor   (if known)

SCHEDULE E - CREDITORS HOLDING UNSECURED PRIORITY CLAIMS
(Continuation Sheet)

_____
TYPE OF PRIORITY

CREDITOR'S NAME AND MAILING ADDRESS INCLUDING ZIP CODE	CODEBTOR	HUSBAND, WIFE, JOINT, OR COMMUNITY	DATE CLAIM WAS INCURRED, NATURE OF LIEN, AND DESCRIPTION AND MARKET VALUE OF PROPERTY SUBJECT TO LIEN	CONTINGENT	UNLIQUIDATED	DISPUTED	AMOUNT OF CLAIM WITHOUT DEDUCTING VALUE OF COLLATERAL	UNSECURED PORTION, IF ANY
ACCOUNT NO.								
			VALUE $					
ACCOUNT NO.								
			VALUE $					
ACCOUNT NO.								
			VALUE $					
ACCOUNT NO.								
			VALUE $					
ACCOUNT NO.								
			VALUE $					
ACCOUNT NO.								
			VALUE $					

Sheet no. ____ of ____ sheets attached to Schedule of Creditors
Holding Priority Claims

Subtotal
(Total of this page)

Total
(Use only on last page of the completed Schedule E.)

(Report total also on Summary of Schedules)

In re_____   Case No._____
                Debtor   (if known)

SCHEDULE F - CREDITORS HOLDING UNSECURED NONPRIORITY CLAIMS

State the name, mailing address, including zip code, and account number, if any, of all entities holding unsecured claims without priority against the debtor or the property of the debtor, as of the date of filing of the petition. Do not include claims listed in Schedules D and E. If all creditors will not fit on this page, use the continuation sheet provided.

If any entity other than a spouse in a joint case may be jointly liable on a claim, place an "X" in the column labeled "Codebtor," include the entity on the appropriate schedule of creditors, and complete Schedule H-Codebtors. If a joint petition is filed, state whether husband, wife, both of them, or the marital community may be liable on each claim by placing an "H", "W", "J", or "C" in the column labeled "Husband, Wife, Joint, or Community."

If the claim is contingent, place an "X" in the column labeled "Contingent." If the claim is unliquidated, place an "X" in the column labeled "Unliquidated." If the claim is disputed, place an "X" in the column labeled "Disputed." (You may need to place an "X" in more than one of these three columns.)

Report total of all claims listed on this schedule in the box labeled "Total" on the last sheet of the completed schedule. Report this total also on the Summary of Schedules.

[ ] Check this box if debtor has no creditors holding unsecured nonpriority claims to report on this Schedule F.

CREDITOR'S NAME AND MAILING ADDRESS INCLUDING ZIP CODE	CODEBTOR	HUSBAND, WIFE, JOINT, OR COMMUNITY	DATE CLAIM WAS INCURRED AND CONSIDERATION FOR CLAIM. IF CLAIM IS SUBJECT TO SETOFF, SO STATE.	CONTINGENT	UNLIQUIDATED	DISPUTED	AMOUNT OF CLAIM
ACCOUNT NO.							
ACCOUNT NO.							
ACCOUNT NO.							
ACCOUNT NO.							

_____continuation sheets attached

Subtotal [_____]
Total [_____]

(Report total also on Summary of Schedules)

In re_____ Case No._____
        Debtor   (if known)

SCHEDULE F - CREDITORS HOLDING UNSECURED NONPRIORITY CLAIMS
(Continuation Sheet)

CREDITOR'S NAME AND MAILING ADDRESS INCLUDING ZIP CODE	CODEBTOR	HUSBAND, WIFE, JOINT, OR COMMUNITY	DATE CLAIM WAS INCURRED AND CONSIDERATION FOR CLAIM. IF CLAIM IS SUBJECT TO SETOFF, SO STATE.	CONTINGENT	UNLIQUIDATED	DISPUTED	AMOUNT OF CLAIM
ACCOUNT NO.							
ACCOUNT NO.							
ACCOUNT NO.							
ACCOUNT NO.							
ACCOUNT NO.							
ACCOUNT NO.							
						Subtotal	

Sheet no. _____ of _____ sheets attached to Schedule of Creditors
Holding Nonpriority Claims

(Report total also on Summary of Schedules)

In re_____   Case No._____
                   Debtor   (if known)

SCHEDULE G - EXECUTORY CONTRACTS AND UNEXPIRED LEASES

Describe all executory contracts of any nature and all unexpired leases of real or personal property. Include any timeshare interests. State nature of debtor's interest in contract, i.e. "Purchaser," "Agent," etc. State whether debtor is the lessor or lessee of a lease. Provide the names and complete mailing addresses of all other parties to each lease or contract described.

NOTE: A party listed on this schedule will not receive notice of the filing of this case unless the party is also scheduled in the appropriate schedule of creditors.

[ ] Check this box if debtor has no executory contracts or unexpired leases.

NAME AND MAILING ADDRESS, INCLUDING ZIP CODE, OF OTHER PARTIES TO LEASE OR CONTRACT.	DESCRIPTION OF CONTRACT OR LEASE AND NATURE OF DEBTOR'S INTEREST. STATE WHETHER LEASE IS FOR NONRESIDENTIAL REAL PROPERTY. STATE CONTRACT NUMBER OF ANY GOVERNMENT CONTRACT.

In re_____   Case No._____
                        Debtor   (if known)

SCHEDULE H - CODEBTORS

Provide the information requested concerning any person or entity, other than a spouse in a joint case, that is also liable on any debts listed by debtor in the schedules of creditors. Include all guarantors and co-signers. In community property states, a married debtor not filing a joint case should report the name and address of the nondebtor spouse on this schedule. Include all names used by the nondebtor spouse during the six years immediately preceding the commencement of this case.

☐ Check this box if debtor has no codebtors.

NAME AND ADDRESS OF CODEBTOR	NAME AND ADDRESS OF CREDITOR

In re_____   Case No._____
                    Debtor   (if known)

SCHEDULE I - CURRENT INCOME OF INDIVIDUAL DEBTOR(S)

The column labeled "Spouse" must be completed in all cases filed by joint debtors and by a married debtor in a chapter 12 or 13 case whether or not a joint petition is filed, unless the spouses are separated and a joint petition is not filed.

Debtor's Marital Status:	DEPENDENTS OF DEBTOR AND SPOUSE		
	NAMES	AGE	RELATIONSHIP

Employment:	DEBTOR	SPOUSE
Occupation		
Name of Employer		
How long employed		
Address of Employer		

Income: (Estimate of average monthly income)	DEBTOR	SPOUSE
Current monthly gross wages, salary, and commissions (pro rate if not paid monthly)	$_____	$_____
Estimated monthly overtime	$_____	$_____
SUBTOTAL	$_____	$_____
LESS PAYROLL DEDUCTIONS		
a. Payroll taxes and social security	$_____	$_____
b. Insurance	$_____	$_____
c. Union dues	$_____	$_____
d. Other (Specify:_____)	$_____	$_____
SUBTOTAL OF PAYROLL DEDUCTIONS	$_____	$_____
TOTAL OF NET MONTHLY TAKE HOME PAY	$_____	$_____
Regular income from operation of business or profession or farm (attach detailed statement)	$_____	$_____
Income from real property	$_____	$_____
Interest and dividends	$_____	$_____
Alimony, maintenance or support payments payable to the debtor for the debtor's use or that of dependents listed above.	$_____	$_____
Social security or other government assistance (Specify)_____	$_____	$_____
	$_____	$_____
TOTAL MONTHLY INCOME	$_____	$_____

TOTAL COMBINED MONTHLY INCOME $_____   (Report also on Summary of Schedules)

Describe any increase or decrease of more than 10% in any of the above categories anticipated to occur within the year following the filing of this document:

In re_____   Case No._____

Debtor   (if known)

SCHEDULE J - CURRENT EXPENDITURES OR INDIVIDUAL DEBTOR(S)

Complete this schedule by estimating the average monthly expenses of the debtor and the debtor's family. Pro rate any payments made bi-weekly, quarterly, semi-annually, or annually to show monthly rate.

☐ Check this box if a joint petition is filed and debtor's spouse maintains a separate household. Complete a separate schedule of expenditures labeled "Spouse".

Rent or home mortgage payment (include lot rented for mobile home) .... $_____

Are real estate taxes included?   Yes____ No____

Is property insurance included?'   Yes____ No____

Utilities   Electricity and heating fuel .... $_____

                Water and sewer .... $_____

                Telephone .... $_____

                Other _____ $_____

Home maintenance (repairs and upkeep) .... $_____

Food .... $_____

Clothing .... $_____

Laundry and dry cleaning .... $_____

Medical and dental expenses .... $_____

Transportation (not including car payments) .... $_____

Recreation, clubs and entertainment, newspapers,

magazines, etc. .... $_____

Charitable contributions .... $_____

Insurance (not deducted from wages or included in home mortgage payments)

      Homeowner's or renter's .... $_____

      Life .... $_____

      Health .... $_____

      Auto .... $_____

      Other_____ $_____

Taxes (not deducted form wages or included in home mortgage payments)

Specify_____ $_____

Installment payments: (In chapter 12 and 13 cases, do not list payments to be included in the plan)

      Auto .... $_____

      Other_____ $_____

      Other_____ $_____

Alimony, maintenance, and support paid to others .... $_____

Payments for support of additional dependents not living at your home .... $_____

Regular expenses from operation of business, profession, or farm (attach detailed statement) $_____

Other_____ $_____

TOTAL MONTHLY EXPENSES (Report also on Summary of Schedules) .... $_____

[FOR CHAPTER 12 AND 13 DEBTORS ONLY]

Provide the information requested below, including whether plan payments are to be made bi-weekly, monthly, annually, or at some other regular interval.

A.   Total projected monthly income .... $_____

B.   Total projected monthly expenses .... $_____

C.   Excess income (A minus B) .... $_____

D.   Total amount to be paid into plan each_____ $_____

(interval)

In re_____   Case No._____
            Debtor   (if known)

DECLARATION CONCERNING DEBTOR'S SCHEDULES

DECLARATION UNDER PENALTY OF PERJURY BY INDIVIDUAL DEBTOR

I declare under penalty of perjury that I have read the foregoing summary and schedules,

consisting of _____sheets, and that they are true and correct to
            (Total shown on summary page plus 1)

the best of my knowledge, information, and belief.

Date_____   Signature:_____
                                                    Debtor

Date_____   Signature:_____
                                              (Joint Debtor, if any)

                             [If joint case, both spouses must sign.]

Penalty for making a false statement or concealing property: Fine of up to $500,000 or imprison-
ment for up to 5 years or both. 18 U.S.C. §§ 152 and 3571.

In re_____   Case No._____
              Debtor   (if known)

STATEMENT OF FINANCIAL AFFAIRS

This statement is to be completed by every debtor. Spouses filing a joint petition may file a single statement on which the information for both spouses is combined. If the case is filed under chapter 12 or chapter 13, a married debtor must furnish information for both spouses whether or not a joint petition is filed, unless the spouses are separated and a joint petition is not filed. An individual debtor engaged in business as a sole proprietor, partner, family partner, or self-employed professional, should provide the information requested on this statement concerning all such activities as well as the individual's personal affairs.

Questions 1 - 15 are to be completed by all debtors. Debtors that are or have been in business, as defined below, also must complete Questions 16 - 21. Each question must be answered. If the answer to any question is "None", or the question is not applicable, mark the box labeled "None." If additional space is needed for the answer to any question, use and attach a separate sheet properly identified with the case name, case number (if known), and the number of the question.

DEFINITIONS

"In business." A debtor is "in business" for the purpose of this form if the debtor is a corporation or partnership. An individual debtor is "in business" for the purpose of this form if the debtor is or has been, within the two years immediately preceding the filing of this bankruptcy case, any of the following: an officer, director, managing executive, or person in control of a corporation; a partner, other than a limited partner, of a partnership; a sole proprietor or self-employed.

"Insider." The term "insider" includes but is not limited to: relatives of the debtor; general partners of the debtor and their relatives; corporations of which the debtor is an officer, director, or person in control; officers, directors, and any person in control of a corporate debtor and their relatives; affiliates of the debtor and insiders of such affiliates; any managing agent of the debtor. 11 U.S.C. § 101(30).

1.   Income from employment or operation of business.

None
☐

State the gross amount of income the debtor has received from employment, trade, or profession, or from operation of the debtor's business from the beginning of this calendar year to the date this case was commenced. State also the gross amounts received during the two years immediately preceding this calendar year. (A debtor that maintains, or has maintained, financial records on the basis of a fiscal rather than a calendar year may report fiscal year income. Identify the beginning and ending dates of the debtor's fiscal year.) If a joint petition is filed, state income for each spouse separately. (Married debtors filing under chapter 12 or chapter 13 must state income of both spouses whether or not a joint petition is filed, unless the spouses are separated and a joint petition is not filed.)

AMOUNT   SOURCE (if more than one)

2.   Income other than from employment or operation of business.

None   State the amount of income received by the debtor other than from employment, trade, profession, or operation of the debtor's business
☐   during the two years immediately preceding the commencement of this case. Give particulars. If a joint petition is filed, state income for each
        spouse separately. (Married debtors filing under chapter 12 or chapter 13 must state income for each spouse whether or not a joint petition is
        filed, unless the spouses are separated and a joint petition is not filed.)

AMOUNT   SOURCE

---

3.   Payments to creditors

None a.   List all payments on loans, installment purchases of goods or services, and other debts, aggregating more than $600 to any creditor,
☐   made within 90 days immediately preceding the commencement of this case. (Married debtors filing under chapter 12 or chapter 13 must include
         payments by either or both spouses whether or not a joint petition is filed, unless the spouses are separated and a joint petition is not filed.)

NAME AND ADDRESS OF CREDITOR	DATES OF PAYMENTS	AMOUNT PAID	AMOUNT STILL OWING

None b.   List all payments made within one year immediately preceding the commencement of this case to or for the benefit of creditors who
☐   are or were insiders. (Married debtors filing under chapter 12 or chapter 13 must include payments by either or both spouses whether or not
         a joint petition is filed, unless the spouses are separated and a joint petition is not filed.)

NAME AND ADDRESS OF CREDITOR AND RELATIONSHIP TO DEBTOR	DATE OF PAYMENT	AMOUNT PAID	AMOUNT STILL OWING

---

4.   Suits, executions, garnishment and attachments

None a.   List all suits to which the debtor is or was a party within one year immediately preceding the filing of this bankruptcy case. (Married
☐   debtors filing under chapter 12 or chapter 13 must include information concerning either or both spouses whether or not a joint petition is filed,
         unless the spouses are separated and a joint petition is not filed.)

CAPTION OF SUIT AND CASE NUMBER	NATURE OF PROCEEDING	COURT AND LOCATION	STATUS OR DISPOSITION

177

None b.   Describe all property that has been garnished or seized under any legal or equitable process within one year immediately preceding the commencement of this case. (Married debtors filing under chapter 12 or chapter 13 must include information concerning property of either or both spouses whether or not a joint petition is filed, unless the spouses are separated and a joint petition is not filed.)

NAME AND ADDRESS OF PERSON FOR WHOSE BENEFIT PROPERTY WAS SEIZED	DATE OF SEIZURE	DESCRIPTION AND VALUE OF PROPERTY

---

5.   Repossessions, foreclosures and returns

None   List all property that has been repossessed by a creditor, sold at a foreclosure sale, transferred through a deed in lieu of foreclosure or returned to the seller, within one year immediately preceding the commencement of this case. (Married debtors filing under chapter 12 or chapter 13 must include information concerning property of either or both spouses whether or not a joint petition is filed, unless the spouses are separated and a joint petition is not filed.)

NAME AND ADDRESS OF CREDITOR OR SELLER	DATE OF REPOSSESSION, FORECLOSURE SALE, TRANSFER OR RETURN	DESCRIPTION AND VALUE OF PROPERTY

---

6.   Assignments and receiverships

None a.   Describe any assignment of property for the benefit of creditors made within 120 days immediately preceding the commencement of this case. (Married debtors filing under chapter 12 or chapter 13 must include any assignment by either or both spouses whether or not a joint petition is filed, unless the spouses are separated and a joint petition is not filed.)

NAME AND ADDRESS OF ASSIGNEE	DATE OF ASSIGNMENT	TERMS OF ASSIGNMENT OR SETTLEMENT

None b.   List all property which has been in the hands of a custodian, receiver, or court-appointed official within one year immediately preceding the commencement of this case. (Married debtors filing under chapter 12 or chapter 13 must include information concerning property of either or both spouses whether or not a joint petition is filed, unless the spouses are separated and a joint petition is not filed.)

NAME AND ADDRESS OF CUSTODIAN	NAME AND LOCATION OF COURT CASE TITLE AND NUMBER	DATE OF ORDER	DESCRIPTION AND VALUE OF PROPERTY

7.   Gifts

7.	Gifts

None ☐	List all gifts or charitable contributions made within one year immediately preceding the commencement of this case except ordinary and usual gifts to family members aggregating less than $200 in value per individual family member and charitable contributions aggregating less than $100 per recipient. (Married debtors filing under chapter 12 or chapter 13 must include gifts or contributions by either or both spouses whether or not a joint petition is filed, unless the spouses are separated and a joint petition is not filed.)

NAME AND ADDRESS OF PERSON OR ORGANIZATION	RELATIONSHIP TO DEBTOR, IF ANY	DATE OF GIFT	DESCRIPTION AND VALUE OF GIFT

8.	Losses

None ☐	List all losses from fire, theft, other casualty or gambling within one year immediately preceding the commencement of this case or since the commencement of this case. (Married debtors filing under chapter 12 or chapter 13 must include losses by either or both spouses whether or not a joint petition is filed, unless the spouses are separated and a joint petition is not filed.)

DESCRIPTION AND VALUE OF PROPERTY	DESCRIPTION OR CIRCUMSTANCES AND, IF LOSS WAS COVERED IN WHOLE OR IN PART BY INSURANCE, GIVE PARTICULARS	DATE OF LOSS

9.	Payments related to debt counseling or bankruptcy

None ☐	List all payments made or property transferred by or on behalf of the debtor to any persons, including attorneys, for consultation concerning debt consolidation, relief under the bankruptcy law or preparation of a petition in bankruptcy within one year immediately preceding the commencement of this case.

NAME AND ADDRESS OF PAYEE	DATE OF PAYMENT, NAME OF PAYOR IF OTHER THAN DEBTOR	AMOUNT OF MONEY OR DESCRIPTION AND VALUE OF PROPERTY

10.   Other transfers

None

List all other property, other than property transferred in the ordinary course of the business or financial affairs of the debtor, transferred either absolutely or as security within one year immediately preceding the commencement of this case. (Married debtors filing under chapter 12 or chapter 13 must include transfers by either or both spouses whether or not a joint petition is filed, unless the spouses are separated and a joint petition is not filed.)

NAME AND ADDRESS OF TRANSFEREE; RELATIONSHIP TO DEBTOR	DATE	DESCRIBE PROPERTY TRANSFERRED AND VALUE RECEIVED

11.   Closed financial accounts

None

List all financial accounts and instruments held in the name of the debtor or for the benefit of the debtor which were closed, sold, or otherwise transferred within one year immediately preceding the commencement of this case. Include checking, savings, or other financial accounts, certificates of deposit, or other instruments; shares and share accounts held in banks, credit unions, pension funds, cooperatives, associations, brokerage houses and other financial institutions. (Married debtors filing under chapter 12 or chapter 13 must include information concerning accounts or instruments held by or for either or both spouses whether or not a joint petition is filed, unless the spouses are separated and a joint petition is not filed.)

NAME AND ADDRESS OF INSTITUTION	TYPE AND NUMBER OF ACCOUNT AND AMOUNT OF FINAL BALANCE	AMOUNT AND DATE OF SALE OR CLOSING

12.   Safe deposit boxes

None

List each safe deposit or other box or depository in which the debtor has or had securities, cash, or other valuables within one year immediately preceding the commencement of this case. (Married debtors filing under chapter 12 or chapter 13 must include boxes or depositories of either or both spouses whether or not a joint petition is filed, unless the spouses are separated and a joint petition is not filed.)

NAME AND ADDRESS OF BANK OR OTHER DEPOSITORY	NAMES AND ADDRESSES OF THOSE WITH ACCESS TO BOX OR DEPOSITORY	DESCRIPTION OF CONTENTS	DATE OF TRANSFER OR SURRENDER, IF ANY

13. Setoffs

None ☐ List all setoffs made by any creditor, including a bank, against a debt or deposit of the debtor within 90 days preceding the commencement of this case. (Married debtors filing under chapter 12 or chapter 13 must include information concerning either or both spouses whether or not a joint petition is filed, unless the spouses are separated and a join petition is not filed.)

NAME AND ADDRESS OF CREDITOR	DATE OF SETOFF	AMOUNT OF SETOFF

---

14. Property held for another person

None ☐ List all property owned by another person that the debtor holds or controls.

NAME AND ADDRESS OF OWNER	DESCRIPTION AND VALUE OF PROPERTY	LOCATION OF PROPERTY

---

15. Prior address of debtor

None ☐ If the debtor has moved within the two years immediately preceding the commencement of this case, list all premises which the debtor occupied during that period and vacated prior to the commencement of this case. If a joint petition is filed, report also any separate address of either spouse.

ADDRESS	NAME USED	DATES OF OCCUPANCY

The following questions are to be completed by every debtor that is a corporation or partnership and by any individual debtor who is or has been, within the two years immediately preceding the commencement of this case, any of the following: an officer, director, managing executive, or owner of more than 5 percent of the voting securities of a corporation; a partner, other than a limited partner, of a partnership; a sole proprietor or otherwise self employed.

(An individual or joint debtor should complete this portion of the statement only if the debtor is or has been in business, as defined above, within the two years immediately preceding the commencement of this case.)

16.   Nature, location and name of business

None a.   If the debtor is an individual, list the names and addresses of all businesses in which the debtor was an officer, director, partner, or
☐ managing executive of a corporation, partnership, sole proprietorship, or was a self-employed professional within the two years immediately preceding the commencement of this case, or in which the debtor owned 5 percent or more of the voting or equity securities within the two years immediately preceding the commencement of this case.

b.   If the debtor is a partnership, list the names and addresses of all businesses in which the debtor was a partner or owned 5 percent or more of the voting securities, within the two years immediately preceding the commencement of this case.

c.   If the debtor is a corporation, list the names and addresses of all businesses in which the debtor was a partner or owned 5 percent or more of the voting securities within the two years immediately preceding the commencement of this case.

NAME	ADDRESS	NATURE OF BUSINESS	BEGINNING AND ENDING DATES OF OPERATION

17.   Books, records and financial statements

None a.   List all bookkeepers and accountants who within six years immediately preceding the filing of this bankruptcy case kept or supervised
☐ the keeping of books of account and records of the debtor.

NAME AND ADDRESS	DATES SERVICES RENDERED

None b.   List all firms or individuals who within the two years immediately preceding the filing of this bankruptcy case have audited the books
☐ of account and records, or prepared a financial statement of the debtor.

NAME	ADDRESS	DATES SERVICES RENDERED

None c. List all firms or individuals who at the time of the commencement of this case were in possession of the books of account and records of the debtor. If any of the books of account and records are not available, explain.

NAME   ADDRESS

None d. List all financial institutions, creditors and other parties, including mercantile and trade agencies, to whom a financial statement was issued within the two years immediately preceding the commencement of this case by the debtor.

NAME AND ADDRESS   DATE ISSUED

18. Inventories

None a. List the dates of the last two inventories taken of your property, the name of the person who supervised the taking of each inventory, and the dollar amount and basis of each inventory.

DATE OF INVENTORY   INVENTORY SUPERVISOR   DOLLAR AMOUNT OF INVENTORY
                                                                    (Specify cost, market or other basis)

None b. List the name and address of the person having possession of the records of each of the two inventories reported in a., above.

                                                     NAME AND ADDRESS OF CUSTODIAN
DATE OF INVENTORY   OF INVENTORY RECORDS

19. Current Partners, Officers, Directors and Shareholders

None a. If the debtor is a partnership, list the nature and percentage of partnership interest of each member of the partnership.

NAME AND ADDRESS   NATURE OF INTEREST   PERCENTAGE OF INTEREST

None b.   If the debtor is a corporation, list all officers and directors of the corporation, and each stockholder who directly or indirectly owns, controls, or holds 5 percent or more of the voting securities of the corporation.

NAME AND ADDRESS	TITLE	NATURE AND PERCENTAGE OF STOCK OWNERSHIP

---

20.   Former partners, officers, directors and shareholders

None a.   If the debtor is a partnership, list each member who withdrew from the partnership within one year immediately preceding the commencement of this case.

NAME	ADDRESS	DATE OF WITHDRAWAL

None b.   If the debtor is a corporation, list all officers, or directors whose relationship with the corporation terminated within one year immediately preceding the commencement of this case.

NAME AND ADDRESS	TITLE	DATE OF TERMINATION

---

21.   Withdrawals from a partnership or distributions by a corporation

None   If the debtor is a partnership or corporation, list all withdrawals or distributions credited or given to an insider, including compensation in any form, bonuses, loans, stock redemptions, options exercised and any other perquisite during one year immediately preceding the commencement of this case.

NAME & ADDRESS OF RECIPIENT, RELATIONSHIP TO DEBTOR	DATE AND PURPOSE OF WITHDRAWAL	AMOUNT OF MONEY OR DESCRIPTION AND VALUE OF PROPERTY

[If completed by an individual or individual and spouse]

I declare under penalty of perjury that I have read the answers contained in the foregoing statement of financial affairs and any attachments thereto and that they are true and correct.

Date_____   Signature of Debtor_____

Date_____   Signature of Joint Debtor (if any)_____

[If completed on behalf of a partnership or corporation]

I declare under penalty of perjury that I have read the answers contained in the foregoing statement of financial affairs and any attachments thereto and that they are true and correct to the best of my knowledge, information and belief.

Date_____   Signature_____

_____
Print Name and Title

[An individual signing on behalf of a partnership or corporation must indicate position or relationship to debtor.]

_____ continuation sheets attached

Penalty for making a false statement: Fine of up to $500,000 or imprisonment for up to 5 years, or both. 18 U.S.C. §§ 152 and 3571.

In re_____   Case No._____

Debtor   (if known)

CHAPTER 7 INDIVIDUAL DEBTOR'S STATEMENT OF INTENTION

1. I, the debtor, have filed a schedule of assets and liabilities which includes consumer debts secured by property of the estate.

2. My intention with respect to the property of the estate which secures those consumer debts is as follows:

a. Property to Be Surrendered.

Description of Property	Creditor's name
1. _____	_____
2. _____	_____
3. _____	_____

b. Property to Be Retained. [Check applicable statement of debtor's intention concerning reaffirmation, redemption, or lien avoidance.]

Description of Property	Creditor's Name	Debt will be reaffirmed pursuant to § 524(c)	Property is claimed as exempt and will be redeemed pursuant to § 722	Lien will be avoided pursuant to § 522(f) and property will be claimed as exempt
1. _____	_____	_____	_____	_____
2. _____	_____	_____	_____	_____
3. _____	_____	_____	_____	_____
4. _____	_____	_____	_____	_____
5. _____	_____	_____	_____	_____

3. I understand that § 521(2)(B) of the Bankruptcy Code requires that I perform the above stated intention within 45 days of the filing of this statement with the court, or within such additional time as the court, for cause, within such 45-day period fixes.

Date:_____

_____
Signature of Debtor

UNITED STATES BANKRUPTCY COURT
_____ DISTRICT OF _____

In re_____   Case No._____
                    Debtor   (if known)

CHAPTER 13 PLAN

The debtor shall pay to the trustee out of the debtor's future earnings or other income the sum of $_____ (weekly) (semi-monthly) (monthly). From the funds received the trustee shall make distributions as follows:

1. Expenses of administration and debts entitled to priority under 11 U.S.C. Section 507.

2. Payments to secured creditors whose claims are duly filed and allowed as follows:

3. From the balance remaining after the above payments, dividends to unsecured creditors whose claims are duly filed and allowed as follows:

4. Except as provided in this plan or in the order confirming this plan, upon confirmation of this plan, all property of the estate shall vest in the debtor free and clear of any claim or interest of any creditor provided for by this plan pursuant to 11 U.S.C. Section 1327.

5. [ ] See attached addendum for additional terms.

Dated:_____

_____
Petitioner

_____
Petitioner

Dear Sir or Madam:

YOU ARE HEREBY ADVISED that on _____,
I filed a voluntary petition with the U.S. Bankruptcy Code, you may not:

-Take any action to evict me from my residence.

-Discontinue any service or benefit being provided to me.

-Take any action against me or my property, or repossess any of my property.

Any violation of these prohibitions may constitute contempt of court and be punished accordingly.

Sincerely,

)
)
)
)
vs.   )   Case No. _____
)
)
)
)
)

SUGGESTION OF BANKRUPTCY

The Defendant(s), _____ hereby notifies this Court that said defendant(s) filed a Petition for Bankruptcy, in the United States District Court on _____, a copy of said petition is attached hereto.

Dated: _____   Signed: _____

                                                   Defendant

_____

                                                 Defendant

CERTIFICATE OF SERVICE

I hereby certify that a copy of the foregoing was sent by first class, U.S. Mail on _____, to the following parties:

UNITED STATES BANKRUPTCY COURT
_____ DISTRICT OF _____

In re _____   Case No._____
　　　　　　　Debtor

PROOF OF SERVICE BY MAIL

I, _____ {name}, declare that:

I am over the age of 18 years and am not a party to the within bankruptcy.

I reside, or am employed, in the County of _____ {name of county}, _____ {state}.

My residence/business address is _____ _____.

On _____, 19_____, I served the within _____ _____ {title of document(s) served} by placing a true and correct copy of it (them) in a sealed envelope with first-class postage fully prepaid, in the United States mail at _____ {post office location}, addressed as follows:

I declare under penalty of perjury that the foregoing is true and correct. Executed on _____, 19_____, at _____{city}, _____ {state}.

_____
　　　　　　　Signature

CERTIFIED MAIL

RETURN RECEIPT REQUESTED

No._____

Dear Sir or Madam:

My current financial situation may require me to file for bankruptcy protection. In order to avoid this, I am requesting that my payments on your account be restructured. This will allow me to pay you the full amount you are owed.

My net monthly income is $ _____. After paying essential expenses, such as housing, utilities, food, clothing, transportation for work, and medical expenses, I am left with a monthly disposable income of $ _____. Out of this balance I am able to pay my creditors as follows

CREDITOR	OLD AMOUNT	REVISED AMOUNT

This schedule represents an equal pro-rata reduction for each unsecured creditor. Please let me know if this new arrangement is acceptable. Unless I hear from you before the next payment is due, I will assume this proposal is acceptable, and will make my next payment according to the revised amount.

Thank you for your attention to this matter.

Sincerely,

MONTHLY BUDGET

TOTAL MONTHLY INCOME $\qquad$ $_____

EXPENSES (Monthly):

Mortgage or Rent $_____
Homeowners/Renters Insurance $_____
Real Estate Taxes $_____
Electricity $_____
Gas $_____
Water $_____
Telephone $_____
Garbage Pick-up $_____
Other:_____ $_____
Home Repair/Maintenance $_____
Auto Loan $_____
Other Installment Loan Payments:

_____ $_____
_____ $_____
_____ $_____
_____ $_____
_____ $_____

Auto Insurance $_____
Gasoline $_____
Auto Repairs/Maintenance $_____
Food $_____
Clothing $_____
Medical, Dental, and Medicines $_____
Life Insurance $_____
Laundry $_____
Recreation/Travel/Entertainment $_____
Education $_____
License Fees, Dues, Memberships $_____
Other Taxes $_____
Other:_____ $_____
_____ $_____
_____ $_____
_____ $_____
_____ $_____

TOTAL MONTHLY EXPENSES $_____

UNITED STATES BANKRUPTCY COURT
_____ DISTRICT OF _____

In re _____   Case No._____
                    Debtor

AMENDMENT COVER SHEET

The Debtor hereby files the attached amended documents, consisting of :

[ ]   Voluntary Petition

[ ]   Summary Of Schedules

[ ]   Schedule(s) _____

[ ]   Statement Of Financial Affairs

[ ]   Chapter 7 Individual Debtor's Statement of Intention

[ ]   Chapter 13 Plan

[ ]   Other_____

UNSWORN DECLARATION UNDER PENALTY OF PERJURY

I, _____ and I, _____, declare under penalty of perjury that the information set forth above, and contained in the attached amended documents, consisting of _____ pages, is true and correct to the best of my (our) information and belief.

Dated:_____

_____
                                    Debtor

_____
                                    Debtor's Spouse

UNITED STATES BANKRUPTCY COURT
_____ DISTRICT OF _____

In re _____   Case No._____

MOTION TO CONVERT TO CHAPTER 7

The Debtor, having originally filed this action pursuant to Chapter 13 of the U.S. Bankruptcy Code, hereby moves this court to convert this action to a proceeding pursuant to Chapter 7 of the U. S. Bankruptcy Code. In furtherance of this motion the Debtor has attached a Chapter 7 Individual Debtor's Statement of Intention.

Dated:_____

_____
Petitioner

_____
Petitioner

ORDER

IN CONSIDERATION of the foregoing motion of the Debtor,

IT IS HEREBY ORDERED, that this action is converted to a proceeding pursuant to Chapter 7 of the U. S. Bankruptcy Code.

Dated:_____   _____
Judge

INDEX

A

abandonment of property, 82
administrative fee, 60
after bankruptcy, 91
Alabama, 99
Alaska, 100
alimony, 28, 35, 83
alternatives to bankruptcy, 38
amending forms, 85
Amendment Cover Sheet, 85, 195
Application to Pay Filing Fee in Installments, 60, 78, 158
Arizona, 62, 101
Arkansas, 31, 97, 102
art works, 33
assets, *See* property.
attorneys, 11, 17
automatic stay, 80
automobile loans, 26, 29, 36
automobiles, *See* motor vehicles.
avoiding bankruptcy, 25
avoiding liens, 74, 86

B

bank accounts, 30, 31, 32, 52
bankruptcy alternatives, 38
Bankruptcy Code, 6
bankruptcy courts, 56
Bankruptcy Reporter, 53, 54
Bible, 5
blue book, 33
boats, 29, 30, 32
bonds, *See* stocks.
books, 33

budget, 40
business property, *See* tools of trade.

C

California, 62, 103
cash, 31, 32
CDs, 31, 52
Certificate of Mailing, 86, 192
certificates of deposit, *See* CDs.
Chapter 7 bankruptcy, 6, 14
Chapter 7 Individual Debtor's Statement of Intention, 58, 73, 78, 186
Chapter 11 bankruptcy, 6
Chapter 12 bankruptcy, 6
Chapter 13 bankruptcy, 6, 14
Chapter 13 Plan, 58, 74, 78, 187
checking accounts, *See* bank accounts.
child support, 28, 35, 83
clerk, 7, 10, 57, 77, 79
clothing, 30, 32
codebtors, 65, 70
codes, 53
coin collections, 33
collections, 33
Collier Bankruptcy Manual, 54
Collier Forms Manual, 54
Colorado, 105
community property, 62, 63, 65
Connecticut, 31, 87, 97, 106
Constitution, 5
Consumer Credit Counseling Service, 39
contingent debts, 66
converting to Chapter 7 case, 15, 86
copyrights, 33
corporations, 6, 17

co-signed debts, 14, 76
court judgments, 36
courts, *See* bankruptcy courts.
credit cards, 26, 29, 35, 36, 41, 93
credit counseling, 38, 39
creditors, 10, 15, 41, 81
creditors' meeting, 13, 81

D

debt consolidation loans, 38
debt counselors, 38
debts, 12, 29, 52
Debt Worksheet, 35, 36, 65, 155
Declaration Concerning Debtor's Schedules, 58, 72,
    78, 175
Delaware, 107
disability benefits, 28
discharge, 13, 83
dischargeable debts, 35, 37
dismissal, 14
disputed debts, 66
district courts, *See* bankruptcy courts.
District of Columbia, 31, 97, 108
dividends, *See* stocks.
doubling exemptions, 96

E

effects of bankruptcy, 25
emotional effects of bankruptcy, 26
employers, 26, 27
equity, 33
ERISA (Employee Retirement Income Security
    Act) benefits, *See* retirement benefits.
evictions, 25
evidence, rules of, 7
executory contracts, 69
exempt property, 12, 30, 31, 37, 46, 64
expenses, 71

F

farmers, 6, 17
Federal Bankruptcy Exemptions, 31, 32, 34, 63, 64,
    95, 97
Federal Non-Bankruptcy Exemptions, 31, 64, 89,
    95, 98
fee simple, 61
filing, 79
filing by mail, 79
filing fees, 60, 79
    amount, 60
    paying in installments, 60
    waiver of, 60

final discharge, *See* discharge.
financial effects of bankruptcy, 25
financing statement, 36
firearms, 33
Florida, 34, 109
foreclosure, 25, 43
forms, 55, 151
forms, amending, 85
forms, instructions,
    form-1, 27
    form-2, 29
    form-3, 36
    form-4, 58
    form-5, 60
    form-6, 71
    form-7, 61
    form-8, 62
    form-9, 64
    form-10, 65
    form-11, 67
    form-12, 68
    form-13, 69
    form-14, 70
    form-15, 70
    form-16, 71
    form-17, 72
    form-18, 72
    form-19, 73
    form-20, 74
    form-21, 76
    form-22, 80
    form-23, 88
    form-24, 86
    form-25, 42
    form-26, 91
    form-27, 85
    form-28, 86
fraud, 36, 47, 83
future interest, 62

G

Georgia, 110

H

Hawaii, 31, 97, 111
hearings, 13, 83
home equity, 30
home equity loans, 29, 38
home improvement loans, 29
homeowners insurance, 29
homestead, 34
household goods and furnishings, 30, 32, 52

I

Idaho, 62, 112
Illinois, 34, 113
Income and Expense Worksheet, 27, 37, 40, 51, 91, 153
income taxes, *See* taxes.
income, 28, 49, 70
Indiana, 114
installment loans, 29
insurance, 29, 30, 33
interest income, 28
internet information sources, 54
Iowa, 115
IRA accounts, 52

J

jewelry, 32, 52
judgments, 36, 87
judges, 8, 9

K

Kansas, 116
Kentucky, 86, 117

L

lawsuits, 88
lawyer referral service, 19
lawyers, *See* attorneys.
leases, 69
legal aid, 60
legal research, 53
letter notifying creditors, 80, 190
letter to creditors, 42, 193
licenses, 33
lien avoidance, 86
life estate, 61
life insurance, 30, 33
limitation on filing, 11, 26
Louisiana, 62, 86, 118

M

mail, filing by, 79
Mailing Matrix, 76, 78, 81, 189
Maine, 119
market value, *See* value.
married debtor filing separately, 17
Maryland, 86, 120
Massachusetts, 31, 97, 121
medical bills, 45
Michigan, 31, 97, 122
Minnesota, 31, 97, 123

Mississippi, 86, 124
Missouri, 125
Montana, 126
Monthly Budget, 91, 194
mortgage foreclosure, 25
mortgages, 26, 29, 50
Motion to Convert to Chapter 7, 86, 196
motor vehicles, 26, 30, 32, 51

N

Nebraska, 127
Nevada, 62, 128
new debts, 45
New Hampshire, 129
New Jersey, 31, 34, 97, 130
New Mexico, 31, 62, 97, 131
New York, 132
non-dischargeable debts, 13, 35
non-exempt property, 12, 30, 31, 46, 47
nonpriority claims, 68
North Carolina, 133
North Dakota, 134

O

obtaining credit after bankruptcy, 25, 92
Ohio, 135
Oklahoma, 136
Oregon, 137

P

paintings and art, 33
partnerships, 6, 17
patents, 33
Pennsylvania, 31, 97, 138
pensions, *See* retirement benefits.
personal property, 30, 62
petition, *See* Voluntary Petition.
practice manuals, 54
priority claims, 67
property, 11, 29, 51
property taxes, 29
property value, *See* value.
Property Worksheet, 29, 31, 64, 154

Q

QDRO (Qualified Domestic Relations Order), 90

R

reaffirming a debt, 73, 88
real estate, 30, 32, 51, 61
real estate income, 28

real estate taxes, 28
recreational vehicles, 30, 32
redemption, 73, 87
relatives, sales to, 48
rental income, 28
renters' insurance, 29
repossession, 26, 43
retirement benefits, 8, 26, 28, 30, 52, 89, 96
Rhode Island, 31, 97, 139
rules of evidence, 7

S

Schedule A, 58, 61, 78, 160
Schedule B, 58, 62, 78, 161
Schedule C, 58, 64, 78, 164
Schedule D, 58, 65, 78, 165
Schedule E, 58, 67, 78, 167
Schedule F, 58, 68, 78, 169
Schedule G, 58, 69, 78, 171
Schedule H, 58, 70, 78, 172
Schedule I, 58, 70, 78, 173
Schedule J, 58, 71, 78, 174
secured debts, 12, 31, 35, 36, 37, 65, 73, 74, 75, 87
self-employment, 28
self-help law books, 1
set-offs, 69
six-year limitation on filing, 11, 26
social security, 28, 30
South Carolina, 31, 97, 140
South Dakota, 141
sports equipment, 33
stamp collections, 33
state exemptions, 31, 32, 34, 64, 99
Statement of Financial Affairs, 58, 72, 78, 176
stocks, 28, 33, 52
student loans, 35, 83
Suggestion of Bankruptcy, 88, 191
Summary of Schedules, 58, 71, 78, 159
support, 28

T

take home pay, 28
taxes, 28, 36, 67, 83
Tennessee, 87, 142
Texas, 31, 62, 87, 97, 143
tools of trade, 30, 33
trustee, 10, 13, 25, 81, 82

U

U.S. Constitution, 5
unemployment benefits, 28, 30
unexpired leases, 69
unliquidated debts, 66
unsecured debts, 12, 36, 41, 67, 68, 75
Utah, 87, 144
utilities, 25, 50

V

vacation homes, 30
vacation loans, 29
value, of property, 33, 64
vehicles, *See* motor vehicles.
Vermont, 31, 97, 145
Virginia, 146
Visa, *See* credit cards.
Voluntary Petition, 13, 57, 58, 78, 85, 156

W

waiver of filing fees, 60
Washington, 31, 62, 87, 97, 147
wedding rings, 32
welfare benefits, 28, 30
West Virginia, 148
Wisconsin, 31, 62, 97, 149
workers' compensation, 30
Wyoming, 150

Your #1 Source for Real World Legal Information...

LEGAL SURVIVAL GUIDES™

- Written by lawyers
- Simple English explanation of the law
- Forms and instructions included

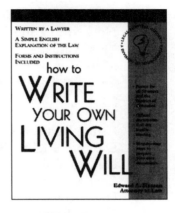

THE POWER OF ATTORNEY HANDBOOK (3RD EDITION)

It is now easier than ever to authorize someone to act on your behalf for your convenience or necessity. Forms with instructions are included, as well as a state-by-state reference guide to power of attorney laws.

140 pages; $19.95;
ISBN 1-57071-348-0

HOW TO FILE YOUR OWN DIVORCE (3RD EDITION)

A step-by-step guide for obtaining a divorce in all 50 U.S. states and the District of Columbia. Includes forms with instructions and explains property division, child support, child custody and visitation, alimony, court procedures, and much more.

240 pages; $19.95;
ISBN 1-57071-224-7

HOW TO WRITE YOUR OWN LIVING WILL

A simple guide for writing living wills in all 50 states and the District of Columbia. Includes official documents that are legally binding, and a step-by-step guide to filling out the documents yourself.

160 pages; $9.95;
ISBN 1-57071-167-4

See the following order form for books written specifically for California, Florida, Georgia, Illinois, Massachusetts, Michigan, Minnesota, New York, North Carolina, Pennsylvania, and Texas! *Coming in 1999: Ohio!*

What our customers say about our books:

"It couldn't be more clear for the lay person." —R.D.

"I want you to know I really appreciate your book. It has saved me a lot of time and money." —L.T.

"Your real estate contracts book has saved me nearly $12,000.00 in closing costs over the past year." —A.B.

"...many of the legal questions that I have had over the years were answered clearly and concisely through your plain English interpretation of the law." —C.E.H.

"If there weren't people out there like you I'd be lost. You have the best books of this type out there." —S.B.

"...your forms and directions are easy to follow." —C.V.M.

Legal Survival Guides are directly available from the publisher, or from your local bookstores.
For credit card orders call 1–800–43–BRIGHT, write P.O. Box 372, Naperville, IL 60566,
or fax 630-961-2168

LEGAL SURVIVAL GUIDES™ NATIONAL TITLES
Valid in All 50 States

LEGAL SURVIVAL IN BUSINESS

How to Form Your Own Corporation (2E)	$19.95
How to Form Your Own Partnership	$19.95
How to Register Your Own Copyright (2E)	$19.95
How to Register Your Own Trademark (2E)	$19.95
Most Valuable Business Legal Forms You'll Ever Need (2E)	$19.95
Most Valuable Corporate Forms You'll Ever Need (2E)	$24.95
Software Law (with diskette)	$29.95

LEGAL SURVIVAL IN COURT

Crime Victim's Guide to Justice	$19.95
Debtors' Rights (3E)	$12.95
Defend Yourself Against Criminal Charges	$19.95
Grandparents' Rights	$19.95
Help Your Lawyer Win Your Case	$12.95
Jurors' Rights (2E)	$9.95
Legal Malpractice and Other Claims Against Your Lawyer	$18.95
Legal Research Made Easy (2E)	$14.95
Simple Ways to Protect Yourself From Lawsuits	$24.95
Victims' Rights	$12.95
Winning Your Personal Injury Claim	$19.95

LEGAL SURVIVAL IN REAL ESTATE

How to Buy a Condominium or Townhome	$16.95
How to Negotiate Real Estate Contracts (3E)	$16.95
How to Negotiate Real Estate Leases (3E)	$16.95
Successful Real Estate Brokerage Management	$19.95

LEGAL SURVIVAL IN PERSONAL AFFAIRS

How to File Your Own Bankruptcy (4E)	$19.95
How to File Your Own Divorce (3E)	$19.95
How to Make Your Own Will	$12.95
How to Write Your Own Living Will	$9.95
How to Write Your Own Premarital Agreement (2E)	$19.95
How to Win Your Unemployment Compensation Claim	$19.95
Living Trusts and Simple Ways to Avoid Probate (2E)	$19.95
Most Valuable Personal Legal Forms You'll Ever Need	$14.95
Neighbor vs. Neighbor	$12.95
The Power of Attorney Handbook (3E)	$19.95
Simple Ways to Protect Yourself from Lawsuits	$24.95
Social Security Benefits Handbook (2E)	$14.95
Unmarried Parents' Rights	$19.95
U.S.A. Immigration Guide (3E)	$19.95
Guia de Inmigracion a Estados Unidos	$19.95

Legal Survival Guides are directly available from the publisher, or from your local bookstores.

For credit card orders call 1–800–43–BRIGHT, write P.O. Box 372, Naperville, IL 60566,
or fax 630-961-2168

LEGAL SURVIVAL GUIDES™ ORDER FORM

BILL TO:		SHIP TO:	
Phone #	**Terms**	**F.O.B.** Chicago, IL	**Ship Date**

Charge my: ☐ VISA ☐ MasterCard ☐ American Express

☐ **Money Order or Personal Check**

| | | | | | | | | | | | | | | | | | | | | |

Credit Card Number

Expiration Date

Qty	ISBN	Title	Retail	Ext.
		LEGAL SURVIVAL GUIDES NATIONAL TITLES		
_____	1-57071-166-6	Crime Victim's Guide to Justice	$19.95	_____
_____	1-57071-342-1	Debtors' Rights (3E)	$12.95	_____
_____	1-57071-162-3	Defend Yourself Against Criminal Charges	$19.95	_____
_____	1-57248-001-7	Grandparents' Rights	$19.95	_____
_____	0-913825-99-9	Guia de Inmigracion a Estados Unidos	$19.95	_____
_____	1-57248-021-1	Help Your Lawyer Win Your Case	$12.95	_____
_____	1-57071-164-X	How to Buy a Condominium or Townhome	$16.95	_____
_____	1-57071-223-9	How to File Your Own Bankruptcy (4E)	$19.95	_____
_____	1-57071-224-7	How to File Your Own Divorce (3E)	$19.95	_____
_____	1-57071-227-1	How to Form Your Own Corporation (2E)	$19.95	_____
_____	1-57071-343-X	How to Form Your Own Partnership	$19.95	_____
_____	1-57071-228-X	How to Make Your Own Will	$12.95	_____
_____	1-57071-331-6	How to Negotiate Real Estate Contracts (3E)	$16.95	_____
_____	1-57071-332-4	How to Negotiate Real Estate Leases (3E)	$16.95	_____
_____	1-57071-225-5	How to Register Your Own Copyright (2E)	$19.95	_____
_____	1-57071-226-3	How to Register Your Own Trademark (2E)	$19.95	_____
_____	1-57071-349-9	How to Win Your Unemployment Compensation Claim	$19.95	_____
_____	1-57071-167-4	How to Write Your Own Living Will	$9.95	_____
_____	1-57071-344-8	How to Write Your Own Premarital Agreement (2E)	$19.95	_____
_____	1-57071-333-2	Jurors' Rights (2E)	$9.95	_____
_____	1-57248-032-7	Legal Malpractice and Other Claims Against...	$18.95	_____
_____	1-57071-400-2	Legal Research Made Easy (2E)	$14.95	_____
_____	1-57071-336-7	Living Trusts and Simple Ways to Avoid Probate (2E)	$19.95	_____
_____	1-57071-345-6	Most Valuable Bus. Legal Forms You'll Ever Need (2E)	$19.95	_____
_____	1-57071-346-4	Most Valuable Corporate Forms You'll Ever Need (2E)	$24.95	_____
_____	1-57071-347-2	Most Valuable Personal Legal Forms You'll Ever Need	$14.95	_____

Qty	ISBN	Title	Retail	Ext.
_____	0-913825-41-7	Neighbor vs. Neighbor	$12.95	_____
_____	1-57071-348-0	The Power of Attorney Handbook (3E)	$19.95	_____
_____	1-57248-020-3	Simple Ways to Protect Yourself from Lawsuits	$24.95	_____
_____	1-57071-337-5	Social Security Benefits Handbook (2E)	$14.95	_____
_____	1-57071-163-1	Software Law (w/diskette)	$29.95	_____
_____	0-913825-86-7	Successful Real Estate Brokerage Mgmt.	$19.95	_____
_____	1-57071-399-5	Unmarried Parents' Rights	$19.95	_____
_____	1-57071-354-5	U.S.A. Immigration Guide (3E)	$19.95	_____
_____	0-913825-82-4	Victims' Rights	$12.95	_____
_____	1-57071-165-8	Winning Your Personal Injury Claim	$19.95	_____
		CALIFORNIA TITLES		
_____	1-57071-360-X	CA Power of Attorney Handbook	$12.95	_____
_____	1-57071-355-3	How to File for Divorce in CA	$19.95	_____
_____	1-57071-356-1	How to Make a CA Will	$12.95	_____
_____	1-57071-408-8	How to Probate an Estate in CA	$19.95	_____
_____	1-57071-357-X	How to Start a Business in CA	$16.95	_____
_____	1-57071-358-8	How to Win in Small Claims Court in CA	$14.95	_____
_____	1-57071-359-6	Landlords' Rights and Duties in CA	$19.95	_____
		FLORIDA TITLES		
_____	1-57071-363-4	Florida Power of Attorney Handbook (2E)	$9.95	_____
_____	1-57071-403-7	How to File for Divorce in FL (5E)	$21.95	_____
_____	1-57071-401-0	How to Form a Partnership in FL	$19.95	_____
_____	1-57248-004-1	How to Form a Nonprofit Corp. in FL (3E)	$19.95	_____
_____	1-57071-380-4	How to Form a Corporation in FL (4E)	$19.95	_____
_____	1-57071-361-8	How to Make a FL Will (5E)	$12.95	_____

_____ ***Form Continued on Following Page***   **SUBTOTAL** _____

To order, call Sourcebooks at 1-800-43-BRIGHT or FAX (630)961-2168 (Bookstores, libraries, wholesalers—please call for discount)

LEGAL SURVIVAL GUIDES™ ORDER FORM

Qty	ISBN	Title	Retail	Ext.
		FLORIDA TITLES (CONT'D)		
_____	1-57248-056-4	How to Modify Your FL Divorce Judgement (3E)	$22.95	_____
_____	1-57071-364-2	How to Probate an Estate in FL (3E)	$24.95	_____
_____	1-57248-005-X	How to Start a Business in FL (4E)	$16.95	_____
_____	1-57071-362-6	How to Win in Small Claims Court in FL (6E)	$14.95	_____
_____	1-57071-335-9	Landlords' Rights and Duties in FL (7E)	$19.95	_____
_____	1-57071-334-0	Land Trusts in FL (5E)	$24.95	_____
_____	0-913825-73-5	Women's Legal Rights in FL	$19.95	_____
		GEORGIA TITLES		
_____	1-57071-387-1	How to File for Divorce in GA (3E)	$19.95	_____
_____	1-57248-047-5	How to Make a GA Will (2E)	$9.95	_____
_____	1-57248-026-2	How to Start and Run a GA Business (2E)	$18.95	_____
		ILLINOIS TITLES		
_____	1-57071-405-3	How to File for Divorce in IL (2E)	$19.95	_____
_____	1-57071-415-0	How to Make an IL Will (2E)	$12.95	_____
_____	1-57071-416-9	How to Start a Business in IL (2E)	$16.95	_____
		MASSACHUSETTS TITLES		
_____	1-57071-329-4	How to File for Divorce in MA (2E)	$19.95	_____
_____	1-57248-050-5	How to Make a MA Will	$9.95	_____
_____	1-57248-053-X	How to Probate an Estate in MA	$19.95	_____
_____	1-57248-054-8	How to Start a Business in MA	$16.95	_____
_____	1-57248-055-6	Landlords' Rights and Duties in MA	$19.95	_____
		MICHIGAN TITLES		
_____	1-57071-409-6	How to File for Divorce in MI (2E)	$19.95	_____
_____	1-57248-015-7	How to Make a MI Will	$9.95	_____
_____	1-57071-407-X	How to Start a Business in MI (2E)	$16.95	_____
		MINNESOTA TITLES		
_____	1-57248-039-4	How to File for Divorce in MN	$19.95	_____
_____	1-57248-040-8	How to Form a Simple Corporation in MN	$19.95	_____
_____	1-57248-037-8	How to Make a MN Will	$9.95	_____
_____	1-57248-038-6	How to Start a Business in MN	$16.95	_____

Qty	ISBN	Title	Retail	E
		NEW YORK TITLES		
_____	1-57071-184-4	How to File for Divorce in NY	$19.95	_
_____	1-57071-183-6	How to Make a NY Will	$12.95	_
_____	1-57071-185-2	How to Start a Business in NY	$16.95	_
_____	1-57071-187-9	How to Win in Small Claims Court in NY	$14.95	_
_____	1-57071-186-0	Landlords' Rights and Duties in NY	$19.95	_
_____	1-57071-188-7	New York Power of Attorney Handbook	$19.95	_
		NORTH CAROLINA TITLES		
_____	1-57071-326-X	How to File for Divorce in NC (2E)	$19.95	_
_____	1-57071-327-8	How to Make a NC Will (2E)	$12.95	_
_____	0-913825-93-X	How to Start a Business in NC	$16.95	_
		PENNSYLVANIA TITLES		
_____	1-57071-177-1	How to File for Divorce in PA	$19.95	_
_____	1-57071-176-3	How to Make a PA Will	$12.95	_
_____	1-57071-178-X	How to Start a Business in PA	$16.95	_
_____	1-57071-179-8	Landlords' Rights and Duties in PA	$19.95	_
		TEXAS TITLES		
_____	1-57071-330-8	How to File for Divorce in TX (2E)	$19.95	_
_____	1-57248-009-2	How to Form a Simple Corporation in TX	$19.95	_
_____	1-57071-417-7	How to Make a TX Will (2E)	$12.95	_
_____	1-57071-418-5	How to Probate an Estate in TX (2E)	$19.95	_
_____	1-57071-365-0	How to Start a Business in TX (2E)	$16.95	_
_____	1-57248-012-2	How to Win in Small Claims Court in TX	$14.95	_
_____	1-57248-011-4	Landlords' Rights and Duties in TX	$19.95	_

SUBTOTAL THIS PAGE ___

SUBTOTAL PREVIOUS PAGE ___

Illinois residents add 6.75% sales tax
Florida residents add 6% state sales tax plus applicable discretionary surtax ___

Shipping— $4.00 for 1st book, $1.00 each additional ___

TOTAL ___

m8286TN
74